SUCCESS *for* EVERYONE

Follow the 7-Step Universal Success Cycle to realise Wealth and Abundance and the Life of your Dreams

ALSO AVAILABLE FROM HANS BEUMER

THE ULTIMATE HAPPINESS SERIES

THE GLOBAL TRAVELLER SERIES

Visit www.hansbeumer.com

THE ULTIMATE HAPPINESS SERIES

SUCCESS *for* EVERYONE

Follow the 7-Step Universal Success Cycle to realise Wealth and Abundance and the Life of your Dreams

HANS BEUMER

Hans Beumer Publications
2016

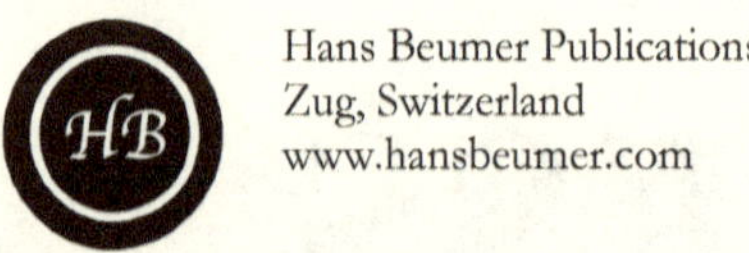

Hans Beumer Publications
Zug, Switzerland
www.hansbeumer.com

Cover designed by Nikita Beumer
Cover Icons designed by Freepik from www.flaticon.com
Edited by Audrey Beumer

First edition published in October 2016:

This book is available as:
-Paperback: ISBN 978-3-906861-11-1
-EBook: ISBN 978-3-906861-12-8

Printed and distributed by Lulu Press, Inc.

CONTENTS

FOREWORD

Everyone wants to achieve their life's goals. Yet, many people fail to achieve success and are unable to realise their life's goals. Many people think small, and as a result set small goals and consequently tie themselves to a small life. Not that small is bad. If you find your passion and happiness in that small life, then you are successful, and you don't need to look any further. Thinking small is only bad when you actually want to achieve something great, but your own thinking convinces you that you won't be able to be successful. Many people dream about finding their passion and happiness in a big way. They dream about big houses, expensive cars and six-figure jobs. They dream about finding a cure for illnesses, being an astronaut, reducing environmental pollution, predicting an earthquake, writing a bestselling novel, designing the newest I-product, making the computer network safe against intruders, etc. Often, however, these big dreams stay dreams, and strongly contradict the small size of the goals that such person sets for him- or herself.

But you too can be successful in achieving your dream life, when you are willing to put in the effort. You have already taken the first important step towards a positive change by reading this book. As with achieving any goal in your life, of course, you need clarity, courage, determination, and persistence. When you consistently follow the 7-Step Universal Success Cycle in this book, success will surely come to you.

I hope that this book inspires you to pursue and achieve success in achieving your life's goals, so that you soon reach your Ultimate Happiness level.

Read to advance your life,
drs. Hans Beumer
October 2016

WHAT YOU WILL LEARN ABOUT SUCCESS

EVERYONE CAN BE SUCCESSFUL

Everyone wants to be successful
But not everyone is successful
There is a certain way to do things
That either leads to success or non-success
This book reveals the certain way that leads to success

- - - - -

Success means many things to many people
But they all have one thing in common
It is the achievement of a goal

- - - - -

Anyone can do what they are passionate about
Anyone can live the purpose in their life
Anyone can be in a loving relationship
Anyone can reach their life's fulfilment
Anyone can be what they want to be
Anyone can achieve their goals
Anyone can become rich
Anyone can be famous
Anyone can be happy
Anyone can be successful

- - - - -

Have you given up without trying to be successful?
Stop making excuses and take control over your life
Have you tried and stopped progressing to further success?
Overcome your fears and make a reset of your goals
Use this book to embark on a self-improvement programme
Which will guide you to your life's biggest success story

- - - - -

STEP 1
DESIRES AND PASSION ARE THE BASIS FOR ALL SUCCESS

Goals should be based on desires
Desires should be based on passions
You have to love what you are doing
Then you will work harder, try harder, and be more persistent
Find your passions, live them and you will be successful
Love what you are doing and all actions will be effortless

- - - - -

You are the originator of creative thought
Which makes you the sole source for your own goals
And initiator of actions to achieve those goals
Therefore, success can only be determined by you

STEP 2
SETTING PURPOSEFUL GOALS

A goal is an objective, something you set out to achieve
It is a dream you intend to bring into the reality of your daily life
Goals need to be concrete, simple, unambiguous, explicit
Write them down and give them a deadline
Set goals that are challenging but attainable
Set multiple goals, one for each major aspect in your life
Let your goals become part of you
Visualise them, meditate on them
Let them become an integral part of your everyday thinking

- - - - -

Frustration, Rejection, Disappointment
May keep you from setting big goals
But there is nothing wrong with these feelings
You can expect them
And all successful people have them
Know that they are only temporary feelings

Let your passion determine the size of your goal
And keep your goals big

- - - - -

Self-Actualisation is about finding your life's goal
Finding your passion in life and pursuing it
Your purpose in life should relate to a cause greater than oneself
It should be for the benefit of others
To generate a lasting positive impact on the life of others
Improve the life of other people

- - - - -

You can't print money; it needs to come from other people
Money is only a means of exchange; it needs to flow
Money flowing to you is only the effect
The cause is the service or product you provide to other people
The effect (money) can never be your primary goal
It has to be the value added to other people
Money may be a short-term motivator
But only passion and desires are long-term motivators

- - - - -

There is a hierarchy of goals
Goals at the lowest level only impact you
Goals at the highest level impact many other people
When these are rooted in the creative mind
And you provide added value over the offered price
Monetary premiums flow back to you
Accumulating in your wealth

- - - - -

Only when your goals are big, will you achieve big success
With small thinking, you will never achieve big goals
As you progress through life and achieve goal after goal
You need to think big, bigger and then biggest
Your biggest goal is not having more money
It must be linked to the purpose in your life
Biggest success is improving the life of as many people as you can

- - - - -

Focus is how much mental- and action attention your goal receives
Focus too little, and you won't get anywhere
Focus too much and you may get obsessed
Obsession may cause loss of balance and all other things in life
Find the right level of focus for your life's goal
But keep the focus on your other goals in perspective as well

- - - - -

Commitment to your goals
Is reflected in your persistence and determination
Both are rooted in passion and belief
Prioritise everything you do
And do only those things that progress you towards your goals

STEP 3
BELIEVING IN SUCCESS

The strength of your belief determines
Why, how, when and how much
Of your goals you expect to be realised
Expect it all, and you will achieve it all

- - - - -

The source of your belief may be weak or strong
Strengthen your source
Through goal setting and focused actions
And your belief will show you the way to success

- - - - -

Harness the power of your belief
Believe in success and you will succeed

As your conscious and subconscious mind
Will find ways to realise your belief
You are what you think you are
When you believe you are successful, you will be successful

- - - - -

Think failure and you will fail
Think success and you will succeed
Consciously use the law of attraction
By thinking positively about your goal achievement
And you will achieve your goals

- - - - -

Strengthen your belief in success
Accept that there are certain events over which you have no control
Don't listen to the disbelief of other people
Each day express gratitude for each progression towards your goals
Meditate to focus your mind on success
Eliminate self-limiting behaviours and beliefs
Think about what you want; don't think about what you don't want
Use visualisation in the achievement of your goals
Discard negative thoughts when they arise
Focus on all past and present success in your life
Think of ways to become even more successful
Look for positive aspects in each negative event
Reflect on yourself and what you are thinking
Don't be concerned with judgment of others
Don't measure yourself against others

- - - - -

Control your minds
Let your conscious mind reprogram your subconscious mind
Direct what goes into both your minds
Don't let any thoughts of failure enter your minds
Focus your minds on your goals and success
Let your subconscious mind work out solutions for you

STEP 4
TAKING CONSISTENT AND FOCUSED ACTIONS

Don't wait for the right time, right circumstances before you act
These will never occur
Have the courage to make a start in uncertain conditions
Regardless of how good your idea is, if you don't act
It will always stay an idea
Only actions can turn an idea into a pot of gold
Start your action to success now

- - - - -

Set up a step-by-step action plan
Write it out, and keep track of your progress
Your detailed plan regulates your progression
Gives you direction, prepares you for the actions
Focuses your energy and keeps you attached to your goal
Your detailed plan shouldn't be too rigid
And does not need to resolve all problems before they happen

- - - - -

Talking does not move you forward
Doing does
You need to take action day after day to make your goal a reality
Procrastination is a goal killer
Each day you must do whatever you can do that day
It is the efficiency and effectiveness of your actions that count
Not the number of hours you put in
Taking action every day keeps your goal in your thoughts
It keeps your focus on the purpose of your life

- - - - -

Success does (not necessarily) need hard work
You need to work smart: efficient and effective
Use the Pareto Principle, instead of perfection
In the competitive field success is achieved by working harder
In the creative field this is structurally different
As you can work on something without competition
This is the only way to become super successful and wealthy

- - - - -

Success is bound by rules of Ethics
In achieving successful goal achievement
Don't take away things from other people
Give added value to other people

- - - - -

The world is continually progressing and developing
You can only be successful when you progress as well
Invest in your self-improvement, and become a better you
Get the required education, experience, knowledge and training
Read one inspirational book every two months
Give this priority over activities that don't help you advance

- - - - -

Your success depends on the cooperation with other people
So align them with your grand vision
Engage people with the right mental attitude
Maintain high standards for yourself and other people
Invest in your people
Share the successes with your people

STEP 5
OVERCOMING OBSTACLES TO SUCCESS

Be like bamboo
Every day work hard to grow (your successes)
When a storm (obstacle) comes, bend with the wind
But never give up and don't let it break you
Each obstacle or period of bad times contains
Learning opportunities and
Business opportunities
For those willing to see them

- - - - -

The way you think about obstacles determines whether you are able to overcome them.
Think that it is not possible and you will fail
Think that it is possible and you will succeed
Think in terms of solutions instead of problems
Don't think about problems when they are unlikely
Think positive and keep faith

- - - - -

There are two sorts of future obstacles
Those that occur and those that don't
Don't let those that may never occur influence your today's actions in becoming successful
For those that could occur
Plan and take concrete actions to avoid them
Think positively that you will overcome them

- - - - -

Overcome existing obstacles in front of you
Predominantly think about the solution, not the problem
Understand the reason why something is happening
Find the positive in a bad situation or problem

Tell yourself there is a solution
Never think of giving up, bar those thoughts
Be persistent but try different solutions if needed
Tackle problems one by one, don't get overwhelmed
Zoom out of the details and take distance
See the bigger picture to get a good solution
Don't get bogged down by mistakes
Find compensation for your limitations

- - - - -

Many obstacles only exist in your mind
They do not exist in your outside environment
They are self-created and are only present within you
Excuses of age, health, luck, money, education or intelligence
They are rooted in fear for failure
Rationalise away all your fears and take action
Find your passion and you will overcome fears

- - - - -

Everything happens for a reason
Though you don't always understand the reason
Karma represents uncontrollable events
Outside your observable influence
The stronger your goals and your actions
The weaker the influence of Karma
On your progression towards success

- - - - -

Many people never see success because they give up
Persistence means having the willpower to pull through
It means being determined never to quit
It means being flexible to adjust to changing circumstances
When times are difficult and obstacles block your way

STEP 6
MEASURING AND REVIEWING PROGRESS

Systematically measure and review your progress
Take timely corrective actions when progress is lagging
Look at new ways to do something better, think creatively
You can't be too rigid and block yourself from new ideas

- - - - -

When you meet an obstacle, don't stall
Keep your momentum by building on other actions
That move you closer to your goal
Momentum may be lost by distractions or loss of focus
Refocus and keep your eye on the big prize
Keep doing all you can to progress towards your goal

STEP 7
ACHIEVING SUCCESS

Chemicals in the brain cause the feelings of success
They generate positive, pleasurable, exciting feelings
Success feelings are good and you can have more of these
Feelings of success or failure are the effect
The cause is your thinking
Think only positively and generate success feelings

- - - - -

Recognise successes
Determine intermediate milestones
To increase your frequency of celebrations
As this will strengthen your goal energy and focus
And give you pleasurable feelings of happiness

- - - - -

Success never comes from your efforts only
Other people contribute to your success
Acknowledge them and share your successes with them
Share your success through charity as well
And more success will come to you
It is the law of attraction at work

- - - - -

Luck is not a determinant factor in your success
As luck does not exist
Putting in hard work for preparations
And seizing the right opportunities bring success

- - - - -

Create the appearance of success
Let other people think you are already successful
Dress for style, quality and show first class
Think of yourself as already successful
Show and talk success in your job appearance
Show other people your positivity
And your appearance will become reality

- - - - -

Success seldom comes overnight
It may take 10, 15, 20 years or a lifetime
It is worthwhile to strive for a goal that may take that long
When this goal reflects your ultimate purpose in life
And captures your all-consuming passion
Giving you energy and drive, so that it seems that time flies

WHEN TO QUIT

Doubts, uncertainties or difficult situations or obstacles
Other people's advice to do something else
None of these are reasons to quit
Only quit when you have lost your passion
When you don't like what you are doing anymore
Or when there is really no other alternative
But then find a new passion, a new purpose in life

THE 7-STEP UNIVERSAL SUCCESS CYCLE

Everyone wants to be successful, but not everyone is
There is a certain way of doing things leading to success or non-success
This Universal Success Cycle reveals the certain way that leads to success

- - - - -

Follow the 7-Step Universal Success Cycle to realise
Wealth and Abundance and the Life of your Dreams

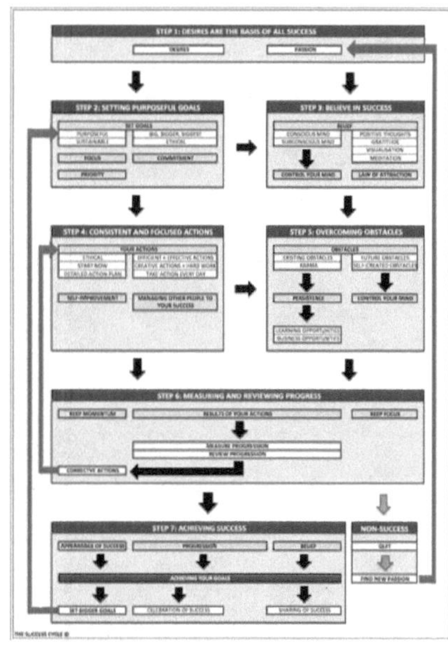

EVERYONE CAN BE SUCCESSFUL

There Is A Certain Way To Do Things

Everyone wants to be successful. The quest for success exists in all age categories, from young to old; in all walks of life, from lower class to upper class; in all races; in all geographical regions of the world; equally in all men and women; in all businesses around the world, whether for non-profit or for profit; in all governments around the world, whether at federal, state, province or county level; in all professions in the world, from carpenter to midwife to investment banker and politician; and so forth. Everyone wants to be successful.

Everyone's drive towards success makes people undertake actions to achieve the success that they desire. Still these actions don't guarantee that success will be achieved. You and your neighbour may be in the same line of business, but still you can be successful, whereas your neighbour is perhaps not. Your siblings may have been raised the same as you, may have received the same education as you, still your siblings may be more successful than you are. Your peers at work may be receiving promotion after promotion, whereas you don't move up the corporate ladder, though you have the same education and working hours. Why does it seem that success favours one person more than the other? Why does it seem that success comes easy to some people whereas others never achieve success despite all their intensive efforts?

One of the main principles of success is that there is enough for anyone who wants it. You can create your own success, and the supply of success (whether it is wealth, relationships, health, time or career) is not limited. The only limitations are those put on oneself, so never think that success is not possible for you; always look at the abundance that is available in the world, and realise that you can create abundance for yourself as well. But it is you who needs to create it, as nobody else will do it for you.

When everyone wants to be successful, but not everyone becomes successful, there must be a certain way of doing things that either leads to success or non-success. The purpose of this book is to analyse the subject of success, identify those key aspects which do lead to success and formulate a simple, methodical and standardised approach which can enable success for everyone.

Everyone wants to be successful
But not everyone is successful
There is a certain way to do things
That either leads to success or non-success
This book reveals the certain way that leads to success

What Is Success?

The first question that should be addressed is: What is success? What does success mean to you? Success means many things to many people. Success could mean closing that $1 million sales contract with your key account, qualifying for entering the College soccer team, catching a 750 lbs. Blue Marlin, giving birth to healthy twin babies, selling your house with a profit, passing that school exam, getting time off from work to take your vacation trip to Hawaii, earning an annual salary of $100'000, passing your driving test, finding your perfect wedding dress, receiving that salary raise, being elected for President of the United States, catching a burglar red-handed, finding your peace in meditation, winning that lawsuit, overcoming cancer, having $1 million on your bank account, owning a Ferrari, etc. I am sure that you can think of many more examples for yourself.

There is one common thread to the question "what is success". It all relates to the achievement of an objective, a goal, a target, an ambition, an aspiration, a hope, a dream, an intention, an idea or an aim.
In mature businesses, objectives and goals are usually defined by a high level of detail, supported by extensive documents and an extremely high level of formalisation. Contrary to businesses, many people do not formalise their personal objectives and goals. Very often these personal goals are based on hopes and dreams, which may only exist in the mind of the person having these hopes and dreams. They may not be documented, they are perhaps not sufficiently defined and analysed, and may lack clarity of vision. The level of formalisation of the objectives, however, is not a guarantor for success either. How many businesses have solid objective

setting and approval processes in place, but still report major misses of their quarterly or annual earnings targets?

The existence of an objective, a goal, a target, an ambition, an aspiration, a hope, a dream, an intention, an idea or an aim is the first key aspect in the Success Cycle. For the purpose of this book, let's capture all these variations of objectives into one word: goal. It is the achievement of a goal that brings success. Goals give meaning and direction to your life. The achievement of meaningful goals is what motivates many people to do the things they do.

Success means many things to many people
But they all have one thing in common
It is the achievement of a goal

Anyone Can Be Successful

Successful people are made up of the same material as you are: flesh, bone, water, fat and organs. Their brain is not bigger than yours. Most successful people are not smarter than you are. Success is not limited to a select few, by some sort of natural selection process. Success does not depend on where you were born, when you were born, or the colour of your eyes, hair or skin. Success is independent of your religion, upbringing, sexual orientation or physical strength. Success is independent of the kind of education that you had. Some people that dropped out of their studies are successful, like Marc Zuckerberg and Bill Gates. Some people who spent many years studying are successful, like Neil deGrasse Tyson and some of the Nobel Prize winners. Some people with physical handicaps become successful, like Jessica Cox and Stephen Hawking, just like people with healthy physical conditions become successful, like Arnold Schwarzenegger and Cindy Crawford. Success is independent of where you live, as people from all countries around the world are successful, whether from a big city or a small town.

Of course the environment has a certain effect on success, as the ability to study will expand the knowledge stored in the brain, when compared to a person who has no possibility to study beyond elementary school. An environment conducive to positive thinking will of course have a positive impact on success, whereas circumstances that only generate negativity and destruction will likely lead to non-success. Similarly, being (geographically or mentally) isolated from other people will make it more difficult to be successful, due to the inherent interdependence on other people and the complexity of the modern day society. Living in a crowded city is, however, not a precondition for success either, as Internet connectivity connects humans even in the most isolated places (such as in space and the arctic). So even when you are 400 kilometers above the Earth's surface in space and you live with only a few other members in the space station, you can still be successful. Look at how the Canadian astronaut Chris Hadfield catapulted his success through his YouTube Videos, while being in the International Space Station.

Those people who are successful focus on the future, they are not hung up on the past. Dwelling on the past means that your mind is focussing on the past. Your past is fixed and cannot be changed anymore, and can therefore never lead to changes. Change is needed to generate success, as success means getting from where you are today (your present state), to where you want to be (your future state). Your past state has no role to play in the process; it is irrelevant. So focus on the future, leave your past for what it is, and you too can be successful. Since this is all in the mind, anyone can do this, so anyone can be successful.

Anyone can do what they are passionate about
Anyone can live the purpose in their life
Anyone can be in a loving relationship
Anyone can reach their life's fulfilment
Anyone can be what they want to be
Anyone can achieve their goals
Anyone can become rich
Anyone can be famous
Anyone can be happy
Anyone can be successful

Where Are You On The Pathway To Success?

For most successful people the path to success resembles a long and winding uphill road with frequent detours and the occasional dead-end. The majority of people never start to traverse this path to success, plenty of people settle for getting only halfway along this path, while only a few complete their path to success.

Let's call this first group of people (Category I) the "given up without trying" category. These people do not move forward in life; they remain where they are. They have limited to no progression in their income, wealth, family relations, social relationships, physical appearance, intellectual development or any other aspect which can be considered under the term of "a successful life". Mainly because of their way of thinking, people in this category stay at one level their whole life. They have mentally capitulated to being stuck in a mediocre life, even though they might have big dreams about a bright future. But in practice they never take any action to chase that big dream. They succumb within the limits of their small life and have a long list of reasons why they are not able to escape the rut of their daily existence. They will rationalise to themselves and anyone who wants to listen to them (spouse, children, parents, co-workers), the reasons why they can't escape their current situation. They will explain extensively that they are really happy where they are, but that their health, age, physical condition, family situation, neighbourhood, weather, long drive to work, absence of a car, absence of savings (or make up any other reasonably sounding situation) prevent them from progressing in their life. But in reality they are not happy, as they silently dream of a different, better, life. Alternatively, some people in this situation will heavily complain about their situation, use the same excuses as mentioned above, but never take the initiative to improve their situation. As they never set a first step on the pathway to success, they will always stay where they are.
Do you know people who are in this category? Are you in this category?

The second category concerns people who did walk the pathway to success, but stopped somewhere along the way. They never completed the path till the very end. We can call them "trying and stopped" (Category II). These people were able to progress their life and achieve intermediate successes to

the fulfilment of their dreams. They successfully traversed the path, but they halted after 10, 15, 20 or 25 years. This group of people also has a rationalisation why they do not continue to progress in their life. They will tell themselves, and their direct environment, that they have already achieved a life which is above average and that they are satisfied with their life and the acquired freedoms. In reality they have developed fears. Their fears for a decline in their current situation, have outgrown their desires to continue their progress. They own a nice house in the suburbs, have two cars, set aside a college fund for their children, and travel for holidays twice a year. Why risk this comfortable life? So the desires for further progression, chasing after the big dream, are put on ice for the benefit of financing college for the children and the longing for (financial) security for the years leading up to retirement. These people then stick it out in well-paid jobs, which have, however, lost their shine and have become a rut at a high level, until they retire.
Do you know people who are in this category? Are you in this category?

The third category of people traverses the pathway to success completely till the end. We can call this category the "successful" (Category III). They are successful because they had a dream, and are now in a situation where they are living their dream. They went the full length of the path to success and had to conquer a long and winding uphill road with frequent detours and the occasional dead-end. But they made it, and are now living their life to the fullest, fulfilling the purpose in their life, living their passion. Their success has provided them with rewards far beyond their expectations and they are sharing these rewards with other people, by giving back to society. They have persisted on their path, never given up, and were always positive that anything is possible with the right attitude. They have worked hard, always believing that their goal is worthwhile achieving, not just for themselves, but for the benefit of the greater good. They are passionate about their job, can't wait for another day to work, radiate happiness and optimism about their future, and stimulate the progression of the lives of many other people. They achieve their goals, and then set even bigger goals to keep them going and progressing in their life, always hungry to do more and better.
Do you know people that are in this category? Are you in this category?

In between Category I and II, and II and III, there is of course one more category. This is the category of people who are consciously travelling on the path to success. Let's call them "trying". Either they are in their early stages on their pathway with still a long way to go (between Category I and

II) or they are well advanced and have the ultimate goal in sight (between Category II and III). This analogy follows a certain timeline linked to a standard career. There are of course exceptions, where people find their passion early in their career, even in their teens, and live their dream for most of their life. As the majority of people will enter into standard career pathways, the above analogy applies to most people. People in the "trying" category still have their eye on the end goal and are generally positive that they will achieve the success that they so desire. Still, they might end up in Category II, or when they are persistent, in Category III.
Do you know people that are in this "trying" category? Are you in this category?

If you are in the first category: stop making up excuses for your present situation, and take control over your life. You have 100 per cent control over your own situation. Change your thinking. On a positive note you are reading this book, and you have already decided that it is time for a change. You are reading this book because you don't yet know how to make the changes to catapult you from Category I to Category II or III. Your past is fixed and cannot be changed anymore. Change is needed to generate success, as success means getting from where you are today (your present situation), to where you want to be (your future situation). So focus on the future, leave your past for what it is, and you too can be successful. Since this is all in the mind, anyone can do this, so anyone can be successful, this includes you. Apply what you are reading in this book and you will be able to move up to another category. Call it your self-improvement programme to become successful.

If you are in the second category, you are facing your life's biggest challenge: can you overcome your fears? It is a really easy decision to stay within the comfort zone of your regular life, with all the financial securities that you have built up. Why put a perfectly controlled life at risk for something that you don't know whether it will succeed? You have worked hard for what you have achieved, and why would you want to put all those efforts at risk? It is much easier to accept your dissatisfaction and complete the ride, than to initiate a goal/success reset. If that is your choice, then be content with it, and you can be proud of what you have achieved and the successes you attained for your employer, your spouse and children, and yourself.
But what if you are not content to be in this category of having given up along the pathway to ultimate success?

Let me apply this to myself. After having been in Category III for many years, I slipped back to Category II. I had walked the pathway to success but stalled after about 20 years into my career. It actually took me another five years to realise that I had stalled, that I needed to do something about the growing dissatisfaction and to find a solution to winning back my passion and reset the goals for my life's success. I had to overcome my fears and scrape all my courage to make the decisions that put me back on the pathway to success. As an Author, I am now traversing a new section on the long and winding road to success. Since I keep moving my goals forward, making them bigger and bigger, this journey will probably take me the rest of my life. I don't mean the rest of my working life till retirement age (a discretionary age set by authorities). When you are living the life of your dreams, when you are living the purpose of your life with passion, that will take you till the end of your life, literally. Look at the many examples of painters, musicians, business moguls, actors and scientists who still work till a very high age, till their soul separates from their body.

What can you do to elevate yourself to the third category? Remember that it is really worthwhile to be in that category, as its rewards are immensely larger than those attained in the second category. Can you re-find your passion? Can your passions grow stronger than your fears?
Have no despair. This book provides guidance. It builds on my personal experience to make the jump from Category II to III, validating that the success principles documented in this book have value, as they sustained the practice test. It is the purpose in my life to share these success principles with you, so that you may also improve your life to Category III.

If you are in the third category: congratulations! You are already living your dream, finding passion in what you do every day, and you have reached your full success potential. I am honoured that you are reading this book. Although there might not be a lot that you can still learn about success, I hope that this book may provide inspiration for setting bigger and even bigger goals, and achieving bigger and even bigger success for the benefit of society at large. Let this book assist you in improving the life of even more people.

If you are in the "trying" category, keep it up; keep pressing on, on the pathway towards your goals. You will only achieve your big success when you never give up. Don't ever quit, and you will be successful and elevate yourself to Category III. Let the success principles in this book guide you to your final destination.

Have you given up without trying to be successful?
Stop making excuses and take control over your life
Have you tried and stopped progressing to further success?
Overcome your fears and make a reset of your goals
Use this book to embark on a self-improvement programme
Which will guide you to your life's biggest success story

The Next Chapters

When success does not depend on where you live, how long and what you have studied, how successful your parents are, how much money you start out with, or what you look like, then what does it depend on? What are the main drivers for becoming successful?

This book provides the answers to those questions. The following chapters identify and analyse the main sources of success. You will read how these sources can best be put to use to maximise your own success. You will obtain concrete guidance to make these principles of success work for you. As the underlying principles for success are the same for everyone, it is possible to capture these principles in a simple, methodical and standardised approach called the 7-Step Universal Success Cycle. The seven steps to success in this cycle are:

Step 1 describes why desires and passions are the basis for all successes. When you do what you love and love what you do, you have a strong basis to becoming successful.
Step 2 introduces you to setting purposeful and sustainable goals. It shows that focus, commitment and prioritisation towards your goals are imperative to becoming successful.

The power of belief is analysed in Step 3. This chapter provides concrete guidance on how to strengthen your belief and control your mind towards success.
Consistent and focused actions are needed to turn your dream into reality. Step 4 analyses several aspects of your actions, including the ethical side, and how to overcome procrastination. Do you know that success does (not necessarily) need hard work?
Many people give up along the way to success because of obstacles and setbacks. Step 5 explains the nature of obstacles and how to overcome them.
Step 6 is about measuring and reviewing progression and how to keep momentum and focus in moving forward towards your goals.
What do you do when you actually achieve your goals and you become successful? Step 7 talks about celebration and sharing of success. This Chapter also explains that luck has nothing to do with success and why it is important to create the appearance of success.

The second last Chapter explains when it is time to quit. Although throughout the book a case is made for never giving up, there are special conditions under which the wise thing to do is quitting your quest for achieving a certain goal.

The Summary Chapter The 7-Step Universal Success Cycle completes the pathway with a graphical visualisation of the principles of success in a flowchart called the 7-Step Universal Success Cycle. Apply this 7-Step Success Cycle to each aspect in your life in which you want to be successful, your relationships, work, money, your life, and you will become successful. The principles are solid and complete and have passed the test of time and practice; it is up to you whether you make them work or not.

Make this book work for you, and work with what this book has to offer you, and you will live the life of your dreams.

STEP 1

DESIRES AND PASSIONS ARE THE BASIS FOR ALL SUCCESS

Do What You Love And Love What You Do

What precedes a goal? What leads a person to setting a goal? Here is where the desires come into play. The human species has progressed throughout the centuries and millions of years, because they desired something better, because they were dreaming big. Humans always had, and still have, grand wishes to evolve themselves, their external conditions, their place amongst the other species and their role and contribution in life. It is this desire that has brought us Wi-Fi, cars, the space shuttle, medicines, etc. From a collective human species perspective desire is good, from a personal perspective desire is good as well, as long as you use it in a positive way, leading you on a path to success when it enables you to reach your goals. Desire without corresponding improvement actions (progression) only lead to status quo. Desires without initiatives to realise those desires always stay dreams.

Desires originate in the nature of the species, always trying to evolve and continue to improve themselves. Species, other than the humans, mostly direct their advancements to their own survival, their physical status. The human species does this as well, but has an additional evolutionary desire. And that is to evolve its environment. The human species has initiated advancement, which has gone far beyond what is necessary for mere survival of the species. It is inherent in the developed human species to keep advancing their physical status and their environment. It seems that each person has a built-in desire towards advancement. In some people these desires are stronger, in others weaker. But everyone has such desires. How each person turns these desires into goals and actions is what creates the big distinction between people. This is what determines whether you are in Category I, II or III.
What are your desires? Are they strong enough that you follow them?

Goals are based on desires, and desires should be based on passion. You have to love what you are doing, because only then you will work harder, try harder, overcome more obstacles and you will be more persistent. Find your passions, live them and you will be successful. Love what you are doing and all actions will be effortless. You won't be able to sleep because of the excitement of working on your goal. You will get up early in the morning before the alarm, because your subconscious mind wakes you up to go to work. Do what you love and you will enjoy life so much more.

Do you do what you love and do you love what you do?

Your desires and passion for something are more important than your talents or level of intellect in the quest for success. It is your strong desire and passion that moves your bum off the couch and puts your body into gear. Your overwhelming desire for a goal makes you undertake all the actions necessary to achieve that goal. An idea without desire is like a seed on infertile grounds. The idea is unlikely to blossom and grow into the reality of your external environment. Having an idea and saying that you will put it into action someday, indicates that the idea is not supported by a strong desire and passion. Someday is then just a code word for never, as the idea stays in your head without flowing down to your heart. In such a case, it is probably the wrong idea anyway. The fruitful ideas that get taken from the dream landscape into the landscape of your external environment are those that are grown out of your desires and passion. So you need to pay attention to the source of the ideas. Those rooted in your own desires are strong ideas. Your passion gives you energy to transform the ideas to concrete things. The ideas with their roots in money, or in the desires of other people, seldom lead to your success.
Do you talk about realising your ideas someday?

Money and reputation are not always good incentives for making a career decision. Though financial security and good reputation are principally good things to have, they don't necessarily mirror desire and passion. Sometimes it is much easier to choose money, a good salary, over a career in an area that one is passionate about. This is particularly the case when the good salary is earned in one's comfort zone, and the area that you are passionate about is riddled with uncertainties. In such cases it is oftentimes an easy decision to choose the money over the passion and desires. In the long run, however, this does not work out well for the person. Happiness will slowly disappear, and is replaced with disappointment, resentment, bitterness and regrets.
Don't you know people who went through such a process? How about you?

Desires can never be about money. It can't be money that fuels your goals. In order to be super successful you have to love what you do. You need to be passionate about your goals to be persistent enough to overcome obstacles and never give up. Your strong desire must be linked to your goal. Never do something just for the money, as in the long-term that will not work. Your long-term goals must be rooted in desires and passions, not in money.

What is your motivation for doing what you are presently doing? Is it the money?

How do you find your passions and desires? Oftentimes it needs trial and error and the courage to experiment, before you arrive on the right track towards your destiny. Some people are lucky and both find and follow their passion from a young age, others may take decades before they start following their passion. Follow your heart and do what you love to do, and you have found your passion. You will know it when you have it.
Have you already found your passion?

Goals should be based on desires
Desires should be based on passions
You have to love what you are doing
Then you will work harder, try harder, and be more persistent
Find your passions, live them and you will be successful
Love what you are doing and all actions will be effortless

Desires Defined By You Or By Others?

For many people other people's desires play an important role in the development of their life. Sometimes other people's desires overshadow one's own desires, as they think they know what is best for you. But success has to be defined by you for yourself. Others can't define it for you. Think about the expectations from parents, family, communities, social networks, teachers, etc. The typical example is when parents have expectations for their children achieving certain goals. Parents want their child to become a lawyer, accountant or doctor, or put their child on piano or violin lessons at the age of 5. Parents want their child to graduate from an Ivy-League College or want their child to be a sports star at high school. Most parents have high expectations of their children, and want their children to be successful. They may want their daughter to be married before becoming 30 years of age and have children by that time. They may want their son to have a good career with life-time employment at a large company and with a large mortgaged house in the suburbs. They may want their children to follow in their footsteps of profession, career, social or economic aspirations. In such cases it is the parents setting the goals for the children, by creating their own expectations of what success means, for their children. When a child deviates from these goals, the parents may easily be tempted to think in terms of non-success or failure on the achievements of their child.

Do you have examples from your own childhood? Does any of this sound familiar?

Only you can take responsibility for your own life. Only you can determine what you want, wherein your passions lie, and what makes you happy. Only you can determine your life's goals. Of course the parents have a determinant role when a child is still very young, and not yet capable of thinking and seeing the longer-term consequences of their goals and actions for themselves. But parents very quickly grow out of that role once their child reaches puberty, when their brain develops their own consciousness for their own future. For some children this process develops already much earlier in life, for some children at puberty, and for some children much later in life. But at some point in time, the parents' determinant role should change to an advisory one as the child takes over their own destiny. At this point in time, the child will set their own goals, find their own purpose in life, while obtaining their own criterion against which to measure success or failure. The parents' influence on the definition of success of the child may linger on for a long time. In case the child has absorbed the goals set by their parents, and genuinely believes that their passion and life's purpose is found in these goals, the goal congruence leads to a consistent definition of success between the parents and the child. Very often, however, such compatibility of goals and definition of success does not occur. Children develop their own interests, their own aspirations, their own passions and thus their own goals for their life. When their own goals deviate from the goals that the parents set for them, the assessment of success might quickly deviate between parents and child. The parents might consider their child to be non-successful because their child's goal deviates from the goals that they have in mind for their child, whereas the child might consider him- or herself successful, because he or she is achieving the goals set by him- or herself.

Are you fulfilling the desires of another person? Is someone else defining what success means for you?

Living up to the desires of another person may make you feel unhappy and miserable when those desires do not match your own. Since this is often the case, these people are not doing what they love to do, and they won't consider themselves successful because they are not chasing after their own dream. There are only two ways out of this: learn to love what you are doing, or change what you are doing. To change what you are doing might mean going against the people you respect and look up to. But you need to do this to take control over your life and develop a life that is based on your own desires and passion. Only then do you stand a good chance of becoming successful according to your own definition of success, instead of someone else's definition. Though the short-term change process might be tough and filled with negative emotions (on both sides), in the long run your investment in the change will pay off for both parties.

The creative and original thought processes about goals, desires and passions arise in the brain of each person, and these creative thought processes steer a person to do what they want to do with their life. Therefore, thoughts of success or failure are directly linked to that person's own thought processes, and thus a person can only decide for himself or herself whether they are successful. Another person can't do this.
Do you let success (and failure) be determined by yourself or someone else?

You are the originator of creative thought
Which makes you the sole source for your own goals
And initiator of actions to achieve those goals
Therefore, success can only be determined by you

STEP 2

SETTING PURPOSEFUL GOALS

Creating Powerful Goals

A goal is an objective, something you set out to achieve. It is a dream you intend to bring into the reality of your daily life. That is why goals need to be concrete, simple, unambiguous, clearly expressed and explicit. When your goal is too complex, difficult to understand, vague, fuzzy or imprecise, you are setting yourself up for failure in achieving that goal. Set your goals against the expectation of a new improved future daily life, and break them down to the lowest level of your daily activities. What will you be doing when you are successful? What will your day look like? Keep it simple and the higher the likelihood that you will be able to move yourself from your current conditions to a future desired situation. You should be able to capture your goal in one sentence of 5 to 10 words. Everything longer is too complex, and sticks less easy in your conscious and subconscious mind. For example: partner in a law firm by Jan 2020; 10 million revenues in my own business by Dec 2018; speak a new language by Jun 2017; become CPA in Oct 2019; own a $1m home by Aug 2021; weigh 150 pounds by end 2016. Quantify your goal (if possible) and the timeline. Do not set your goal as a description of how to get to your desired state, but as the desired state itself. So set as goal to weigh 150 pounds instead of the goal of losing 40 pounds (when you are now weighing 190 pounds). The reason is that the change (losing 40 pounds) from where you are today (190 pounds) to get where you want to be (150 pounds) can never be the goal. The desired situation of where you want to get (150 pounds) has to be the goal.
How do you define your goals? Are they simple, clear and easy to understand?

Set goals that are challenging but attainable, as unrealistic goals will lead to frustration due to non-achievement. The happiness feelings generated by anticipation of reaching a goal usually last much longer than the happiness feelings generated by the goal achievement itself. You could work months or even years to achieve a goal, whereas once the goal is achieved, those happy feelings usually quickly disappear. Revisit your goals regularly, such as once every three months or once a year, or whenever a situation arises that demands a review (e.g. when your life's circumstances change, or when you reach a goal). Three main components drive the creation of the happiness feelings: the satisfaction arising from the realisation of progress towards achieving the goals, the anticipation of what will happen when you achieve the goals, and the sensation from the awareness that the goals themselves are a cause worth pursuing.

Are your goals challenging but attainable? Are you realising happiness from the pursuit of your goals?

Set multiple goals. Your life has many aspects and your involvement in the fast moving society demands that you spread your attention over multiple areas. Such areas relate to your physical state (your health, your body, your vitality), your material state (your career, your financial situation, money, and availability of time), your mind state (your mindfulness) and your spiritual state (the purpose in your life, your care for other people, your relationships and improving the life of other people). You can read more about these four states, and how you can derive happiness from each of these four states, in my book *Happiness for Everyone.* Spread your actions over multiple goals to ensure variation between the main sources of happiness. When one source is exhausted, because you have achieved the goal (or the goal is not attainable anymore) and you haven't set a new one yet, the other sources will keep your happiness level elevated. Multiple goals ensure that you progress in life on multiple fronts. It avoids that your life's progression becomes unbalanced, when it is depending on only one goal. Nobody is that isolated from their environment that they can be super successful based on only one goal. The advancing environment around you requires you setting and keeping multiple goals. Usually there is a hierarchy of goals, with those relating to the improvement of the life of other people at the highest level. Your most important goal should receive the most attention and actions.
Are your goals representing the priorities in your life? Do you have multiple goals?

Your goals have to be about advancement, of yourself and other people. You need to get out of your daily routine, which is killing advancement. You need to do something new in order to progress; don't be stuck in the present. That goal of advancement has to have a good purpose; this means it needs to benefit you and other people at the highest level. Your goals need to represent better future conditions; they must be forward looking. Goals about the past or present, fuelled by revenge, worries, sorrow, despair, melancholy, heartache or grief do not lead to advancement. They will only deepen the negativity in your life, making it a vicious circle from which it is difficult to get out of. Leave the past for what it is, as you can't change it anymore. The present is what it is, as well as, the result of your past goals and actions. A goal can only be about improving the future, for yourself and others. Therefore, see in a goal what can be, and intentionally design positive forward-looking visions in your mind.
Is your goal forward looking, and does it advance you and other people?

Your goals need to be concrete. Only dreaming won't get you anywhere, as a dream is a desire without having the purpose to realise it. You need to be exact about what you want to achieve and by when you want to achieve it. You might not yet know how to achieve your goal, but that is no problem. This will come to you after you set the goal. In order to be as concrete as possible on your goals, write them down. Write them on a piece of paper, write them on a post-it, write them on your white-board, write them in your Moleskine, or write them in your notes on your smartphone or computer. Be as precise as possible for each goal: write down exactly what your goal looks like, describe it in all colours, shapes, sizes, brands, values or other ways. Write down the exact timeline and by when you want to have realised your goal. You have to be specific about your timeline, because this provides the urge to attain that goal. A goal without a specific due date or timeline is a goal which attainment is schedule for "someday", a code word for never. Be specific by when you want to have achieved a goal, and your mind will create the circumstances to put in force the actions needed to achieve that goal at the set date.
Did you write down your goals? Are they detailed enough and do they have a deadline?

After you set your goals, you need to keep them vivid and ever so present in your daily life. Setting a goal and then burying the piece of paper and never thinking about the goal anymore, won't get you towards your goal. You need to keep your goals visible and in your dominant thoughts. When you really, really want something, then your mind will be concentrating on that thing and your thoughts and conversations will be overflowing with this topic. This is a good test of how you identify yourself with your goals. If you have difficulties concentrating on your goals, then either they are not the right goals, or you have too many distractions and you need to remove all the clutter from your life in order to become focused.
Are your goals present in your daily life? Are they dominant, or are you easily distracted from them?

Visualisation of your goals can be done by creating a vision board and putting your vision board in a place in your house where you see it multiple times each day. You can stick it on the fridge, put it in your study, on the bathroom mirror or on the table next to your bed. Consciously visit your goals, during your meditation sessions, your quiet times, your morning rituals, while you are commuting to work, while you are in the traffic jam, while you are jogging, on the treadmill in the fitness studio, or before going to sleep. Let your goals soak in your mind and become an integral part of

your everyday thinking and thoughts. Let your goals become part of you; let them become you. Think about them in detail, create vivid pictures in your mind about your goals, how you will feel once you achieved them, how grand your life will be then, how much happiness will flow from them, how good you will feel, and you will create a lot of positivity and constructive mind power. This positivity and mind power will then find a way to realise your goals.
Do you have the habit of visualising your goals? Do you set time aside to concentrate on your goals?

A goal is an objective, something you set out to achieve
It is a dream you intend to bring into the reality of your daily life
Goals need to be concrete, simple, unambiguous, explicit
Write them down and give them a deadline
Set goals that are challenging but attainable
Set multiple goals, one for each major aspect in your life
Let your goals become part of you
Visualise them, meditate on them
Let them become an integral part of your everyday thinking

Don't Let Rejection, Disappointment And Frustration Keep You From Setting And Maintaining Big Goals

There is nothing wrong in feeling desperate, feeling like giving up, reaching a high level of frustration because of failures, rejections and non-belief of other people. It seems that many very successful people go through such emotions and stages, and it is something to expect.
When you know that you can expect it, you can prepare yourself for it. The worst thing to do, however, would be to never start at all or give up along the way. Even though the time between start and success can be hard, the

point is to start anyway. If you don't start, or quit, it is guaranteed that you'll never achieve success. So start, take that first step and never quit. Let's look at some examples where people set big goals and were able to reach them, despite rejections, disappointments and frustrations along the way to success:

- Steve Jobs: he started Apple Computer at the age of 21 in his parents' garage and continued to follow his passion for computers and software since then. He believed in his products and designs and was convinced that he could change the world. Although his own company Apple ousted him after nine years, he continued to develop his ideas and came back to Apple eleven years later. Indeed, the Apple computers and products significantly changed the way we look at the design and use of computers, mobile music and the mobile telephone, and improved the life of many hundreds of millions of other people.

- JK Rowling: despite being turned down by many publishers for her first book in the Harry Potter series, she kept believing in herself and kept taking actions to achieve her goal of becoming a best-selling author. Before she became famous, she depended on social welfare, while raising a young daughter as a single mom. She believed in her writing and her success eventually came. The topic and her style of writing touched the hearts of hundreds of millions of readers, and together with the movies she provided entertainment to an enormous audience. Had she given up on her belief, her goal and her actions, she would not have sold nearly 500 million copies of her books.

- Jay-Z: he is the living example of the American dream. He was born in poverty in Brooklyn and grew up amongst violence and drugs. At a young age he found his passion for music and despite his difficult home circumstances, and initial difficulties of selling his songs, he never gave up and created many successful businesses in music, clothing and the management of other artists.

- James Dyson: before he started to sell many millions of his bagless vacuum cleaner, he had a tough time making ends meet while he developed thousands of prototypes before he had a working version. Several large vacuum-cleaner manufacturers rejected his product and it took him many more years (when he was in his forties) before he successfully started producing and selling them through his own organisation.

The examples show that all these highly successful people had to deal with rejection, disappointment and frustration before becoming hugely successful. They lived in circumstances of poverty or had troubles to make ends meet. They received rejection from well-established companies, being told that they were lousy at what they were doing or that they would never succeed. They were told off and suggested to give up what they were doing. They were told that they would be better off letting go of their dreams and get a regular salaried job. But these people did none of that. They kept believing in themselves, though at times their belief might have been very thin as well, and did not give up. People around them, such as a wife, a husband, a friend, or parents, supported their belief. So when your belief runs thin, turn to someone close to you to pull you through, but do not give up on yourself. It took all of them hard work, focused and dedicated actions to achieve their goals. They identified their passion, their purpose in life, perhaps after some trial and error, but once they found it, they stuck with it through the difficult times, that somehow always seem to precede the times of success.

Your passion for the purpose in your life will pull you through regardless of any rejections, frustrations and intermediate failures and other negative influences. When your belief in success is rattled, and your actions seem to lead nowhere, you can find strength in knowing that your passion will not waver by temporary setbacks. Once you find the purpose in your life, keep pursuing this, despite the difficulties that you are in and the uncertain outlook. You can build on the knowledge that nothing stays the same, that the only thing that is permanent is change. This means that eventually the times of difficulty will pass and success will come. But it will only come to you when you have not given up in the meantime.
Are you acting like Steve Jobs, JK Rowling, Jay-Z and James Dyson, and never give up on the passion of your life, despite disappointments, rejections and frustration?

Frustration, Rejection, Disappointment
May keep you from setting big goals
But there is nothing wrong with these feelings
You can expect them
And all successful people have them
Know that they are only temporary feelings
Let your passion determine the size of your goal
And keep your goals big

Your Purpose In Life

After work you find yourself sitting on the couch eating a take-out pizza or a microwave meal. You put the kids to bed and spend the remainder of the evening zapping the TV channels. You focus on the weekly sports game or the episode of your favourite TV show. You go to bed without thinking about anything in particular, other than the next day's dull routine. You have no real focus in life, other than making it from pay-check to pay-check and the daily routine both at work and at home. There is little excitement in your life. It is the typical life of a person without any goals.

It is up to you, and only you, to shape your future. You have full control over your own life, and with that over your life's goals and the success towards achieving those goals. It is fully within your own power to get from life what you want. But you have to put in the effort. When you put in no effort, you get nothing in return. When you put in mediocre efforts, you get mediocre returns. When you put in significant efforts, you get significant returns.

All progress in human society is based on people setting purposeful and sustainable goals. People dared to dream of something better and took all the necessary actions to realise their dream. Nobody progresses in life without first setting a goal. People without goals typically don't see much development in their life. They don't know where their life is going and can't seem to free themselves from the shackles of a disappointing, dull and routine daily life. They did not identify, develop or chase after their passions, and blame other circumstances in their life for not being able to make progress. The good news is that it is never too late, as it does not matter where you were or where you are now. The only thing that matters is where you want to get (your goal).

Do you have a vision of your life, its purpose and the destination to be reached, or do you let fate, other people, or your present environment decide where you are heading and do you drift rudderless on the choppy waters of life?

Self-Actualisation is about finding your life's goal, finding your passion in life and pursuing that. At this level, the passion should relate to a cause greater than oneself. It should be for the benefit of others, so the question raised is, how to generate a lasting positive impact on the life of others. The question is easily posed, but the answer might be difficult to find and the answer might shift during your lifetime. Usually a person goes through several stages during their lifetime. At present you are most likely in one of the following stages: being educated in your early years, developing your career, raising and taking care of your family, maturing in your career, or retiring in your late years. During each of these stages, you are following specific stage-related objectives, which fulfil the purpose of your life in that specific stage. Your transition from one stage to the next stage is the ideal time to reassess the purpose of your life.

When you find such purpose, your life will become much easier and far more rewarding. It will probably need risk taking to get out of your comfort zone and identify your true purpose in life. But when you wake up every morning full of energy and exhilaration, then you know that you are on the right path. The ultimate purpose in life is your contribution to the advancement of others. When you improve the life of others, you elevate your own life at the same time, and enduring happiness will be upon you. The world would be such a better place when everybody would be fulfilling the purpose of their life.

Self-actualisation, finding your passion, living the purpose of your life, are as personal as they can get. You are a unique person, one out of 7.5 billion, and there is no one exactly matching your character and passions. The topic of self-actualisation is analysed in detail in my book *Travel Guide to Self-Actualization.* Please review that book for further guidance on finding your true passion in life. Key activities to achieve self-actualisation can be:

- Create awareness that you have an existing situation that needs to be addressed. Support the development of your awareness by reading relevant books on this topic.

- Take time to find what you really like to do, where your passion in life lies. Link your passion to the improvement of the life of other people.

- Make a structured and thoughtful plan to get from where you are today to living the purpose in your life. Put in sufficient planning efforts and carefully consider your decisions before putting them into action. Support your approach with risk assessments, and let your analysis show that it is doable.

- Consistently execute your plan, and transform your life, through goals that are detailed, specified, measurable and have a deadline.

The overall aim is to find and fulfil the purpose in your life, your passion, which will automatically lead to the highest level of happiness. When you live the purpose in your life, your happiness is certain, as it is the only possible outcome. As is often said, live your passion, and you will never work a day in your life.

Self-Actualisation is about finding your life's goal
Finding your passion in life and pursuing it
Your purpose in life should relate to a cause greater than oneself
It should be for the benefit of others
To generate a lasting positive impact on the life of others
Improve the life of other people

Money Can't Be Your Primary Goal

How about setting a specific goal for money? Well, the money goal has two sides.

Firstly, you can't (legally) print money yourself, it needs to come to you from other people. That means that you need to offer something to other people (a service or product), for which they pay you money in return. So money is only a by-product or effect of your offering to other people. Consistent with the law of attraction, if you want to influence the effect (more money), you will have to change the cause (better service or product). If you want to earn a higher salary, you have to deliver a better performance. If you want to charge a higher hourly rate as a consultant, you need to increase your knowledge and experience about the topic. If you want to increase your sales, you have to sell more products, by improving your product, or your sales and marketing efforts. Cause and effect, and more money is always the effect.

Secondly, money is only a means of exchange. Setting a goal for money and then hoarding the money without spending any will not make you happy. When you are just hoarding money your mind will develop fears of losing the money, together with the developing thoughts that you don't have enough money. With the law of attraction at work, your ever-growing fears will actually lead you to losing your money, and you will end up not having enough money. It is in the nature of money that it needs to flow and put to use. It is best put to use for the improvement of the life of other people. When you use the money for good purposes, more money will flow back to you, as you are showing that you have more than enough money. Your state of mind that you have more than enough money will bring more money to you.

The conclusion is to never set money as the primary goal. Your primary goal should always be related to the underlying activity, which gets you the money. You can, however, set money as a secondary goal, linked to the primary goal. For example, you can make it a goal to pass your exam, which will result in you becoming more successful in your job, which will result in an increase in salary. You can make it your goal to successfully complete your big project, as a result of which you will get paid a big bonus. You can make it your goal to complete the development of your new product, as a result of which you will be able to sell it at a price premium in the market, which results in wealth accumulation. You can make it your goal to become CEO of a fortune 500 company, which will enable you to command a certain compensation package, which results in wealth accumulation.

Usually your primary goal is based on your passion. When you stay committed to your passion, money flows to you automatically. It is your passion to become a CEO, which gets you that job. It is your passion for the development of the new product that makes you develop something much better than your competition. It is your passion for the big project that makes you put in all the efforts to complete that project. It is your passion for the subject that you are studying, which makes you pass your exam. Your passion for what you are doing in your daily life is your drive to success. It is your passion that drives your energy level to achieve higher and higher goals, and bigger and bigger successes.

You may desire to accumulate wealth and gain financial independence, but you need to be passionate about the way and the method to achieve this. If you are not passionate about the product or service (the cause), which must result in your wealth accumulation and financial independence (the effect), then you will never achieve this financial goal. This means that purely the money can never be your motivator. When money is your motivation, you are likely going to be frustrated with the service or product (the pathway) somewhere along the way to achieving your goal. In turn this will lead to disappointment because the desired amount of money is not coming your way. It is not coming your way, because your lack of passion for the pathway will develop negative thoughts, fears, doubts, and even resentment for what you are doing. In the end your conscious and subconscious mind will conclude that the goal of money is not attainable, and you will give up and fall back into a rut and a mediocre life again. You will have no sense of purpose, no passion for your daily activities and become a Category I person for the rest of your life. So don't let money drive your long-term goals.

Never do it for the money, because having money as a primary goal never works. Let me give the following example. You might presently be in a job with a caring boss, well-trained subordinates and eco-friendly, interesting products, and kind customers, earning a satisfactory salary of $75'000 per annum. Your primary goal is to enable the success of the company and your customers, through its eco-friendly products in a socially enjoyable work environment. You are satisfied with your salary, but that is not the reason

why you spend so many hours in the office. You work hard to make the company and customers advance. Now picture that you were asked to change division within the company, and your new job pays $150'000. You are super excited about both the doubling in salary and increase in responsibilities. But here is the catch: your bosses only care about themselves and don't give you the support you need, your subordinates are clueless, your customers constantly complain, and the product pollutes the environment. You see that the doubling of your salary is on your pathway to bigger successes (your wealth goal), so you accept the new job. Think about what you can do with all the extra money! A year in the job you are completely frustrated with your bosses, your subordinates, your customers, and the product. You think that the money may be on your pathway to greater wealth, but you don't see where the job itself is leading you to bigger success. Well, the money is good, so you decide to continue in the job by making the money your primary goal. You tell yourself that you are doing this job for the money, as all other sources for motivation have disappeared and you don't consider this job as purposeful to your life anymore. Exactly because of this reason, it won't take long till you decide to ask for a transfer or you resign from the company to go back to a working environment where you have a purpose in an enjoyable setting, even when this means taking a cut in salary. Having money as a primary goal simply does not work in practice. Money does not make one happy. Living a purposeful life in a job that you are passionate about does. Therefore, the primary goal for your success must be related to your purpose in life and something that you are passionate about. Put money as your primary goal and failure to achieve that goal is pre-programmed.
What is your primary goal? Is it money?

A Category I person often has money as their primary goal, because money is simply needed to survive in daily life. A Category III person never has money as a primary goal; their overarching goal is always related to their life's purpose and passion. A category II person did not have money as a primary goal until he halted on his pathway to success, and preserving his money, and the status it brought, became of primary concern.

When you do have (to set) money as primary goal, it is often a reflection that you are in a bad situation, as you need money to simply survive and pay the next bills or debts. From the point of view of success and the law of attraction, this is a very difficult situation, but not one that is insurmountable. The difficulty of the situation is that your mind will be fully occupied with the thoughts of having insufficient money and needing money. It is this line of thinking which makes the money goal an unattainable goal. Thinking that you don't have enough money attracts more situations in which you won't have enough money as the law of attraction, in combination with your subconscious mind, makes sure your predominant thoughts are turned into reality. Persistently think of needing money and you will be in need of money. The only way out of this is to change your thinking, which is probably one of the most difficult catch-22 situations for a Category I person. How can you think that you have an abundance of money, when in reality you are always short on money and debts may be piling up? This is one of the main reasons why many Category I people can't seem to escape that category, and can't seem to move up to Category II or even III. This may, however, also be the reason why a Category II or III person may stay poor when they go bankrupt. Their thinking keeps them locked in. Changing your thinking can be achieved by changing your primary goal: away from (needing) money, to something that helps you advance in your life by improving the life of other people. This does the following for you: you shift yourself away from the shortage of money to a whole different level of a meaningful life. It is this meaningful life that triggers positive thinking, positive results, positive rewards and ultimately success. Money then becomes a positive by-product flowing to you in abundance, enabling you to easily pay all your bills and debts. Money is the effect of doing certain things in a certain way; it is not the cause. The effect can't be a primary goal; the cause has to be the primary goal. As with all successes, they don't come overnight and need efforts and actions. So for a Category I person to shift thinking from needing money to actually having enough money, takes time, hard work and focused actions to be effectuated. Find both purpose and passion in life, be persistent, never give up, think of success, and soon you will find yourself in a situation where money is indeed available in abundance.

Money might work as a motivator in the short-term, but it never works as a motivation for the achievement of mid-term or long-term goals. Your motivation for mid-term and long-term goals must be based on both passion and desires.
What is your main motivation for achieving your short-term goals? Is it money? Is money also the driver for your mid- and long-term goals?

Don't let making money be your primary thought and objective. Instead, think about how you can help other people advance in their life. Think about what service or product you can offer to improve the life of other people. What can be done better, cheaper, easier, and more efficient? How

can you help other people solve their problems? How can you fulfil needs and desires of other people? Let that what you offer as service or product be rooted in your passion, and you will have fun doing those things. Help other people be successful and you will be successful yourself. They will pay you handsomely for your support in their success. The higher your contribution to their success, the more money comes your way. Find out what affects the success of other people and be creative in finding a place for your service or product on the market for success.
Are you helping other people advance in their life or are you only focused on helping yourself advance?

You can't print money; it needs to come from other people
Money is only a means of exchange; it needs to flow
Money flowing to you is only the effect
The cause is the service or product you provide to other people
The effect (money) can never be your primary goal
It has to be the value added to other people
Money may be a short-term motivator
But only passion and desires are long-term motivators

Goals Rooted In The Creative Mind Bring Wealth

What sort of goals do you set? Do you set a goal of making $100'000 or $1'000'000 of income each year, do you set a goal of owning a specific type of car or multiple cars, having a certain type of relationship, recovering from a certain illness, owning a house with 7 rooms in a specific neighbourhood, etc.? There are many sorts of goals, which can be categorised in levels. The lowest levels are the physical and materialistic ones; the higher levels are the mind and the spiritual ones.

There is a hierarchy of goals. At the lowest level you find goals that only relate to your own person. Their reach into society and the life of other people is very limited to absent. Examples of these goals are relating to your physical state or your material state. For example, goals to shed a certain body weight, goals to reach a certain fitness level, goals to have a certain physical appearance, goals to win a marathon running race, goals to overcome a severe illness, goals to earn a certain salary level, goals to own a certain type of house, goals to the size of your bank account, etc. Such goals are purely focussing on yourself, without having a direct impact on other people. When such goals are part of a team goal, then there is a certain reach into the life of other people, as it will take a team effort to realise such a goal. For example, winning a football championship, or growing the profits in a partnership business.

The highest level of goals fully relates to other people. They relate to improving the life of other people. The beauty of this goal is that when you improve the life of other people, you will automatically also improve your own life. Look back to the examples of Steve Jobs, JK Rowling, Jay-Z and James Dyson. They all had big goals far beyond their own person. They had goals to positively impact the life of many millions of other people, through the creative processes of inventions, writing and music. In fact, you can say that many of the most successful people based their success on creativity. This is true for successful musicians, authors, actors, athletes, politicians, inventors, scientists, thinkers and businessmen. Think of any of the super successful people that you admire, and for most of these, their success is rooted in creativity. In this respect, creativity means doing something in a different way than anybody has done before, thereby creating value for other people by offering them something new at a price that is lower than the perceived value to the people buying into the offering.

This means that if you want to define for yourself a goal of improving the life of other people, impacting millions of other people, you have to think of a concept rooted in creativity in order to come up with something, which differs from the present products or services offered on the market. There are numerous examples of the super successful people who all prove that this is possible. It comes back to the creative mind of those successful people, and this creative mind is independent of where you live, what kind of upbringing you received, how long you studied, your race, sexual orientation, gender, or any other factors of your environment. Having the awareness that such success is rooted in the creative mind, gives you the advantage over other people who do not think this way. This is why some people become successful and others not, despite having received the same education, living in the same neighbourhood, having the same age, starting out with the same amount of money. Successful people use their creative mind to create added value to other people. The interesting point is that everybody has a creative mind, and therefore everybody can be successful. But to be successful you need to do certain things in a certain way, as described in this book. Here is where the population is split into the Categories I, II and III.

When you improve the life of other people, you will automatically also improve your own life. But this only happens when you set the improvement of the life of other people as a first goal. In this respect, if you set the improvement of your own life as a first goal, you are unlikely going to achieve the improvement of the life of other people. The reason is that you will focus your efforts and energies on doing what is best for you, instead of doing what is best for society at large. As the reach of your improvements is limited to yourself, and perhaps a few people around you, the law of attraction will give you improvements relating to one person only. When you focus on the improvements for many people, the law of attraction will channel back to you the consequences of improvements for these many people. It is the exponential multiplier effect at work. The more people receive added value from your product or service, the more will be channelled back to you, and thus the more successful will you be.

Be aware that there is a clear sequence to these flows. You first need to add more value to others, before the consequences of these successes flow back to you.

In terms of timelines, the run-up to success may take anywhere from a short time to a very long time. The creative mind of some people identify added value opportunities which are relatively easy to implement and for which other people are relatively easy to convince. This may short-track the run-up to success. These are, however, exceptions. More often, success does not come overnight, and the way to success may take many years. James Dyson is a good example of a long road to success.
When success is finally arriving, it is quite often an explosion, bringing back to you the exponential effects of the added value generated for other people. Look at the example of JK Rowling. Once her books found their way through the distribution channels, within three years, she sold so many copies of her books that her wealth accumulated to hundreds of millions of

dollars. This is of course an exceptional and remarkable success, but it shows that it can be done.

When these people with an ordinary background, in ordinary circumstances, can put their creative mind at work to generate added value for the life of millions of other people, then so can you. Then so can you become super successful at the highest level and accumulate wealth beyond your wildest dreams.

So how wild are your dreams? How long is your run-up to super success? Have you already given up during the run-up, or are you persistent?

The accumulation of wealth beyond your wildest dreams is a positive side-effect of generating added value for other people. If you would put accumulation of wealth as your first and main objective, you are likely going to have a tough time achieving this goal. Wealth can only come to you when other people are willing to make you wealthy. You will never be able to force other people to do this. Other people will only make you wealthy when you offer them something, which is of more value to them than they are paying to you. The point is that you as a single person need to distribute value to many other people, where each other person receives a small portion of added value, which will subsequently trigger a flow back to you. This flow back to you consists in many other people sharing a portion of their added value with you. Because the accumulation of the returns from all these other people converges on one point, namely you, this is how you can become wealthy.

There is a hierarchy of goals
Goals at the lowest level only impact you
Goals at the highest level impact many other people
When these are rooted in the creative mind
And you provide added value over the offered price
Monetary premiums flow back to you
Accumulating in your wealth

Think Big, Bigger and then Biggest

Only when your goals are big, will you achieve big success. With small thinking, you will never achieve big goals. Look at some big accomplishments of humankind in the last 2000 years. The Romans could only create their large empire because they were thinking on a big scale, their empire covering more than 40 countries. The Dom in Cologne, Germany, could only be built because in the year 1248 their architects were dreaming about an enormous cathedral reaching high in the sky. Neil Armstrong was only able to walk on the moon in 1969 because a Nation was thinking big. We now have the Internet, instantly connecting most people on Earth, only because computer scientists at the end of the 1960s were thinking big. These accomplishments were possible because some people had big dreams and set out to realise their big goals. Then other people continued these dreams and dreamt bigger and even bigger. We are now exploring the solar system, have space shuttles and are sending space vehicles into deep space. In 2015, Facebook had almost 1.5 billion active users. Thinking big, setting big goals is the power behind all human accomplishments.

How is your thinking? Are you thinking big?

There is no limit to your thinking; the mind is creative without boundaries. Your mind can conceive thoughts of grandeur, splendour and beauty about anything that you desire. Your thoughts have no limits and can imagine anything. The beauty of the mind is that it can create your desired state in an instant, irrespective of the situation you are in. You may be poor, but your mind can make you think about wealth and riches; your thoughts can take you from rags to riches in a second. Your thoughts can create the most beautiful life for you, such as an abundance of money, million dollar houses, loving family relationships, a career that you are passionate about, luxury cars, long holidays on golden sandy beaches, and everything more you desire in life. It is easy and fun to do, and everybody can do this. Still, only a few people think this big about themselves. Whatever you persistently think about, you will achieve and see reflected in your external conditions. As within, so without. So why are so many people in Category I living dull and mediocre lives? Because they have given up on their dreams, and have shifted their thinking from big to small. When they were young, they must have thought big about their future, expecting a beautiful life ahead of them. But then over the years their parents, teachers, bosses and other societal influences have been persistently telling them what they could and could not do. Intentionally or unintentionally, there are many societal forces at work that keep people and their thinking small. It takes courage, and often times going against the advice of people close to you, to break free from these societal forces. Only you control your mind, only you steer your thinking. Break free from what others expect from you, when these expectations are holding you back. Think your own thoughts of your life, without restrictions, and make those thoughts beautiful, as you would want your life to be. When your thoughts are strong and persistent they set in motion a powerful force. This force is you, everything you want and everything you attract. You can realise in life what you dream of. If you dream small, you will have a small life. If you dream big, you will have a big life. If you dream the biggest, bigger than everyone else, then you will have a life and successes bigger than everyone else. It is really up to you, and you only. So start dreaming big, bigger and then biggest, dream a most beautiful life, dream it with passion and desire. Your goals need to be grand if you want to have a grand life. So make them grand, don't limit yourself. The most common reason for people being in Category I is that they have created self-limiting beliefs. Reality is that there are no limits to what you can achieve in the world, the only limits are those you place in your own mind. So thinking big, bigger and then biggest is a mental attitude which everyone is capable off. You just need to break free from the limitations that you or other people have put on the size of your thinking. You have the power to create your own future as you wish it to be.

Are you using the limitless creative power of your mind? What is your mental attitude towards your goals?

There is of course a difference between idle dreaming, wishful thinking, and actively pursuing your dreams. When your thoughts are persistent, constructive and systematically driven by real passion and desire, then they will impact your external conditions. Your passion and desire should make your thoughts clear, transparent, unchangeable during a consistent period of time. When you want to achieve success, you can only have thoughts of success.

Are you idly dreaming with no intention of doing something about your dreams, or are you actively pursuing them?

As you progress through life and achieve goal after goal, you need to think big, then think bigger and then think even bigger. At each new phase of your life, or at each new level reached, you should set higher and even higher goals. Your biggest goal can't primarily be about having more

money. Your biggest goal has to be about the purpose in your life, which must be linked to improving the life of others. Thinking bigger means thinking about ways to positively impact the lives of even more people than you considered doing before. Your biggest success, your biggest feelings of fulfilment and purpose in life, your highest feelings of the meaning in life, come to you when you are able to positively impact the lives of as many people as you possibly can. Once you achieved a goal, you cannot rest on your laurels. The most successful people keep pushing themselves to bigger and even bigger achievements, they keep moving their boundaries and keep getting out of their comfort zone. They challenge themselves to keep moving forward and doing things better. They keep evolving their dreams, as their life and society develops. The best thing to do for society is to let your goals grow bigger and even bigger. The bigger your goals, the more society will benefit from your achievements. Instead of improving the life of only 10 people, why not improve the life of 100'000 or even 10 million people?
Are you thinking big, bigger and then biggest?

What you dream about will be reflected in your external conditions.
What is your big dream? Is it really big enough, or are you holding back on your dreams because you think, or others say, it is not achievable? What does your life look like in your dreams when you remove all self-imposed limitations?

Only when your goals are big, will you achieve big success
With small thinking, you will never achieve big goals
As you progress through life and achieve goal after goal
You need to think big, bigger and then biggest
Your biggest goal is not having more money
It must be linked to the purpose in your life
Biggest success is improving the life of as many people as you can

Keep Focusing On Your Goals

Focus is both the amount of mental- and action-attention your goal receives. It's both the amount of time in a day you spend thinking about your goal and the amount of time you undertake actions to bring you closer to your goal. The higher your focus, the higher the likelihood that you will be successful in achieving your goal.

100% focus for a short period of time may be needed to keep momentum, to kick-start an intermediate success, to overcome an obstacle or to simply put all your efforts into what you love the most. Maximum focus requires a high level of energy, as your level of concentration is maximised. High focus means shutting out everything else that is not related to your goal.
In the medium- and long-term, 100% focus is not sustainable, neither desirable nor healthy. You might close yourself off to new opportunities, and limit yourself to be open to new pathways to success. You might not take the time to listen to ideas of other people, even though these could lead to opportunities to support your success. You risk a burnout, as the high concentration requires high energy levels, which continuously need to be replenished. You increase the risk of disappointment by losing perspective on the grander scheme of life. Small inconsequential events, circumstances and obstacles may then be easily blown up out of proportion and hurt you more than they should, as you attach too much importance to them. You place a heavy burden on your relationships, as everything is put aside and only your goal achievement counts. Spouse, children, parents and friends will only be able to support such high focus for a limited period of time, until friction arises and problems start to occur. A 100% focus can be very destructive for everything else in your life, and is often a relationship killer. It's then usually called an obsession. While it is fine to obsess about your goal, so that both your passion and love for what you are doing keeps you progressing, you should keep your focus on your goals into perspective. If you let your focus run out of control, you are going to suffer. You might indeed be successful in achieving your goal, but when everything around you in your life has fallen apart, you are not going to be able to enjoy your big prize. What is the value of a big prize, big success, achievement of a big goal, when you have nobody to share it with, when you have destroyed everything else in your life? To be obsessed about achieving your goal is good, as long as you know what you are doing and have the right perspective of your goal and your life. It will give you motivation and

energy to put life into your dreams. Being obsessed with your goal is bad when you lose perspective on the rest of your life and other people suffer because of this. You know that you have a bad obsession when you start acting in unethical ways and want to achieve your goal at any costs, even if it means doing severe damage to your environment and relationships.
Are you already obsessed with your goal? Is that good or bad?

A maximum focus on your goals has both advantages and disadvantages, but so does having too little focus. For example, when you only have let's say a 10% focus, it means that you spend only 10% of your day both thinking about your goal and taking actions to advance towards your goal. A 10% focus is too little and won't get you anywhere. It means that your goal is not your prevailing thought, that you are thinking about all sorts of other things than your goal, and that you undertake hardly any actions to bring you closer to your goal. If you only have a 10% focus on your major goal, it is likely that your thoughts are spread out over many different topics and none of these topics are dominating your mind. Your mind is adrift from topic to topic and is not able to concentrate on a single thing for a longer period of time. You are probably restless and don't know where your life is heading. As a result of these drifting thoughts you probably lack any actions to advance your life and you are stuck in a rut, which you just can't seem to get out of. Sounds familiar? This is the typical pattern for a Category I person. This type of low level focus is a good indicator that such a person hasn't yet found his or her passion. A 10% focus is definitely not enough to become successful.
How much is your focus? Is it enough to be successful?

So what level of focus is required in order to be successful? Is it 50%, 70%, 90% or 100? The topic of success and focus is not an exact science, so it is difficult to pinpoint an exact percentage. However, a certain level of concentration and focus is needed in order to advance towards success. Let's just say that your goal advancement needs to be your dominant thoughts and actions. That means you should probably spend more than two-thirds (66%) of your time thinking, planning and acting towards your main goal, and then you have a good chance of becoming successful. The higher your concentration and focus in the range of 66% to 100%, the higher the likelihood that you will be successful.
Is the focus on your main goal in the range of 66% to 100% of your time?

Your focus is never constant over time. It fluctuates with your life's developments, your circumstances at home, at work or in society, the achievement of successes, the pressures of failures, the size of obstacles put in your way, etc. These fluctuations can go in two directions: You either have a high focus where your focus decreases, or you have a low focus where your focus needs to increase.

When you have consistently had a high focus on your goal, for a long time, but successes did not come, or successes were at the order of the day, you may easily lose focus. Maintaining a high concentration for a long time costs a lot of energy and can become very tiring. When you get tired of always focussing on the same thing, your life may become monotonous, and you can be easily distracted by other things that are going on in your life. An exciting new relationship, a baby being born in the family, a new hobby, or simply taking a break from it all, may take the boredom out of your life. You spread your attention over other things and slowly your focus on your main goal is slipping. It can actually be good to have a temporary slippage as this puts your life back into perspective. It gives you a chance to find new energy or a new energy source, it makes you enjoy other aspects of your life and can cause a newly found balance in your life. But when your attention slips below 50% for longer periods of time, you put your success at risk. You have become side-tracked and need to refocus. Perhaps the side-tracking made you realise that you need to change your main goal or that your passion has shifted to something else.
What did you do when you lost focus?

When you work hard and successes do not come, your focus and concentration on your goal may be slipping as well. You think, why put in all the efforts when you have no results to show for? Your mind starts drifting to other things and then it is easy to get distracted along the way when something interestingly new enters your life. Rather than letting the side-tracking decide where your life is heading, you need to seriously reconsider whether you are chasing the right goal. You need to consider where your passion lies and what the purpose in your life is. Perhaps you will come to the conclusion that indeed you need to focus on a different goal.

When you work hard and you have success after success, you may become complacent. You may think that it is all so easy and everything you touch turns to gold. You may start doing things that are far from your talents and far from your passion, because other people convince you to do so, or because you are bored with your main goal in life. When your successes come too easily, without hardship or obstacles, you are in a very exceptional

situation. You should then set bigger and even bigger goals for yourself instead of getting side-tracked and over-diversify your goals. You may put too many different things on your plate, which may spread your concentration on your main goal too thinly. As a result of over-confidence you spend less and less time and efforts towards concentrating on your main goal. Once your focus falls below a certain level, your successes wane. People start asking, why is this once big superstar not performing anymore? Well, it is because he has lost focus after being spoilt by all the successes.
When you had a high focus once and you let it slip away, it should be relatively easy to regain that high focus. After all, you were used to concentrating on your main goals. A varying focus, from a high- to lower-level, is in itself not so bad, as it gives one a chance to recalibrate on the pathway to success.

Much more difficult is to change a permanently low focus into a high focus. How to get a Category I person to focus like a Category III person? How do you get the mind to focus on one main purpose, while your thoughts are adrift? Passion in combination with overcoming fears are the key to unlocking this kind of focus. It is hard work to concentrate your thoughts and focus your actions on a single large goal. It means that you let go of certain small pleasures and start focusing only on the one big pleasure. Other than being forced to do something like that, the only internal motivator is passion. Find your passion and you will automatically give up on all distractions. Your burning desire, your passion, makes you focus and concentrate all your efforts, thoughts and actions. Get your focus above 66% and you will begin to experience successes. Your successes will propel your motivation to an even higher level of focus, as you want to have more of those good feelings, recognition, rewards and accomplishments.

It is easier to keep focused when times are good, than when times are bad. When times are good, your successes will stimulate you to continue your focus. When you are riding the wave of success, you want to stay on that wave and make it last as long as possible. Though when you are facing bad times, you may be easily distracted. Losing focus is one of the biggest dangers to success, and difficult times make you more susceptible to distractions. When you are rowing your boat of life against the current, it is all too easy to give up and let yourself go with the flow. But if this flow cannot get you anywhere near to where you want to be, it won't contribute to success. Your endeavour might be money consuming, without any pay-off to show for it. People around you may be telling you to quit and put your efforts and money into something else. If you are really passionate

about your goal, then these are all distractions, pulling you away from your main goal. As long as your goal has your passion, and as long as you still believe that there is a way to success, you should keep your focus on your goal and not give in to these distractions. Because in the end you can only be successful when you never quit. Give up, and it will all have been for nothing. Quitting is not an option for the person who wants to be successful.
Are you able to stay focused on your main goal in good times as well as in bad times?

You need to be persistent in your focus in order to be successful. Persistence is based on willpower and self-discipline. You must have the inner urge and self-control to keep doing those things every day that help you progress towards your goals. It is all too easy to live an unplanned life, just doing what you feel like doing every day, without having any long-term goals. Everybody can do that, and a lot of people do. Living from day to day can be extremely relaxing and easy-going, but it can never be fulfilling and meaningful. In order for your life to be meaningful, you need to give it a meaning, and that means defining goals for yourself. Easy to achieve goals will generate only limited feelings of fulfilment. Hard to achieve goals will generate high feelings of fulfilment, just as goals that involve the improvement of the life of other people will have a high meaning. So aim high!
Do you drift from day to day, or do you have the willpower and persistence to focus on your life's goals?

Setting a high goal that is 10 or 20 years in the future will soon lead to loss of focus, because that goal is too far away to keep a continuous focus on a day-to-day basis. You need to break down your life's or long-term goal into more manageable parts or milestones. Set medium-term goals (3 to 5 years), which you need to achieve in order to reach your long-term goals. Then break down those medium-term goals into short-term goals (3 to 12 months). Prepare concrete action plans as to how to achieve these short-term goals and consistently execute these actions every day. Each day, do what you can to progress towards your short-term goals, because each daily progression will equally move you closer to your long-term goal.
This 4-levelled hierarchy for goal setting will help you maintain focus. It is easy to focus on your todays or tomorrows thoughts, efforts and actions, when you have clear transparency how your todays actions support the achievement of your life's big goal, despite it still being 10 or 20 years in the future.

As mentioned before, it is your willpower combined with self-discipline that makes you consistent in undertaking these actions day after day, until the 10 or 20 years have passed and you have attained your big goal and you have become successful. Stay focused and you will be successful.
Did you breakdown your long-term goals into smaller manageable parts?

A strong focus of above 66% does not mean that you shut yourself off from your environment and become intolerable. It does not mean that you become immovable, inadaptable or inflexible. A high focus means that you keep your thoughts and actions focused on your goal. It means that you continually monitor your environment and future for threats and opportunities and that you take all the necessary precautions and preparations to divert threats and seize opportunities. Strong focus on your goals means having a high awareness of everything that relates to your goal achievement.

Equally, a high focus neither means pursuing a goal when you have no passion for it anymore, nor does it mean that your goal does not evolve with you and that you evolve with your goal. Such rigidness is not relating to focus. Like the bamboo, bend with the wind, and when your goal changes, change your focus as well.

Focus is how much mental- and action-attention your goal receives
Focus too little, and you won't get anywhere
Focus too much and you may get obsessed
Obsession may cause loss of balance and all other things in life
Find the right level of focus for your life's goal
But keep the focus on your other goals in perspective as well

Commit To Your Goals And Prioritise

Once you have set clear goals, you need to commit to those goals and prioritise everything you do. In order to be successful in achieving your goals, your goal must be integrated in everything you do. Achieving your goals must become your priority and your passion must generate the power to continuously progress you towards achieving your goals.

Committing to your goal means making your goal part of your life and having the deliberate intention to achieving that goal. Full commitment means that you are willing to do whatever it takes to succeed in achieving your goal, regardless of the time, efforts and resources needed.
Are your goals part of your everyday life?

Your commitment will be strengthened when you keep a vivid picture in mind of the desired outcome, in all colours and details about your life's status and circumstances when you have achieved your goal. Picture it in your mind and experience the feelings of already having reached what you set out to accomplish. Make yourself believe that you have it in the here and now and at present, and act accordingly. Your commitment is the bridge between your beliefs and the realisation of your dreams in your external conditions.
Is your commitment solid enough to build a strong bridge?

One of the most difficult things for a Category I person to do, is to get out of the daily routine of their life and set and commit to goals that advance their life. It takes an enormous commitment to get out of the old habits and pursue challenging new goals. The safety of a boring job, the comfort zone of watching TV each night and the dull daily routines all play negatively into the thoughts of changing your life. These circumstances lead to the thought that tomorrow will be the first day of change towards a new life. But tomorrow never arrives and each new day brings more of the same. You can only overcome these old habits when you commit to a positive advancement in your life. And you need to commit big, otherwise the daily rut will quickly weaken your commitment, and you find yourself postponing changing your life to tomorrow. It is really easy to just keep doing what you have been doing for a long time and to let your past behaviour dictate your future. It takes a huge commitment to turn this around, as it should be your future that determines your present behaviour. Whether your goal is to be a millionaire, become CEO of a fortune 500 company, set up your own company, live in a house on the beach, become a global traveller, or invent a new product, it will never happen if you don't commit to this goal.

Your commitment needs to get you out of your armchair and into new daily routines. You must be committed into putting all the time and efforts needed for achieving your goals and integrating your commitment into everything you are doing, every day, in order to progress towards your goals. You need to reshape your daily priorities around your commitment. Your priorities need to reflect your goals. If your goal is weighing 150 pounds (instead of your current 190 pounds), you must prioritise exercising over sitting on your couch and you must prioritise healthy food over your daily portion of greasy fast food. Your commitment prevents you sitting on the couch the whole evening, by spending time exercising. If your goal is becoming a global traveller, you must prioritise your daily spending budget so that you can save enough money for your world trip. Your commitment must prevent you from spending money on things that you don't really need. If your goal is setting up your own company, you must prioritise creating your own client base and product or service over sitting idly at home, and you must prioritise the use of your resources to focus on becoming self-employed over spending time and money on nice-to-have things. Your commitment influences your decisions on how you develop your daily routines.
Do you prioritise your daily activities towards your main goals?

Your commitment is reflected in the determination and persistence with which you pursue your goals, it is the quality of your dedication toward your goal. The stronger your passion and belief in your goals, the stronger your commitment will be. If you don't enjoy your goal, if it is not your passion, the quality of your dedication will be low, and you won't be successful in achieving it, as you will give up when the first obstacle crosses your pathway. You can easily see the difference between someone who is committed to a cause and someone who is not. The person who is not committed will give up at the first resistance, at the first sign of trouble. They will have all sorts of excuses why it is not going to work, and why they will fail. Their mind is not convinced that they can do it, and the law of attraction will give rise to circumstances that indeed obstruct the achievement of the goal. The person who is not committed gives it a weak non-convincing try to succeed but at the first sign of troubles gives up and tells you "I told you so that it can't be done". His dominant thoughts are that his efforts will fail toward achieving the goal and he puts in only

minimal energy in succeeding. On the other hand, the person who is committed will be persistent and never give up. He will put in all the time and efforts needed to make it work. He has positive thoughts of succeeding and achieving his goal and he will say "I told you so that it can be done". His commitment is based on his passion and belief that he is doing the right thing for the right reason. Strong commitment is rooted in doing what you love and love what you are doing.
Are you one who says that "it can't be done", or that "it can be done"?

Your commitment is a pledge to your future. It gets you from where you are today, to where you want to be. Make your commitment strong by anchoring it in your passion and belief.
What is the source of your commitment? Is it strong enough to get you out of your habitual daily routines?

Commitment to your goals
Is reflected in your persistence and determination
Both are rooted in passion and belief
Prioritise everything you do
And do only those things that progress you towards your goals

STEP 3

BELIEVING IN SUCCESS

You Achieve What You Believe You Can Achieve

Your belief determines why, how, when and how much of your goals you expect to realise through your actions. A strong belief leads to a high expectation and anticipation of your goal achievement. A weak belief causes low expectations for the achievement of your goal. In this respect, belief is defined as an internal expectation or anticipation representing the conviction that the actions will lead to achievement of the goal. If you have a strong belief that you will be successful, you will be successful. If you believe that you will fail, you will fail. A strong belief in success is the basis for all success. The people in Category I "given up without trying" are typically lacking this belief in success. They usually have a strong belief that they will fail, so they don't even start on the pathway to success. The point is that a strong belief (in anything) will trigger the conscious and subconscious mind to find ways to support that belief. If that strong belief is for success, your mind figures out ways to support the achievement of success. Your mind thinks of actions required to achieve the desired success. It will put you in motion to do those things that are needed to reach your goal. If that strong belief is for failure, your mind figures out ways to support the achievement of failure. Your mind makes you inactive, freeze all actions and avoid progress to your goals.

Therefore, the size of your success is directly correlated to the size and strength of your belief in success.

How strong is your belief in success? Do thoughts of failure still occupy your mind? Is your belief in success steadfast or shaken by the smallest commotions?

The strength of your belief determines
Why, how, when and how much
Of your goals you expect to be realised
Expect it all, and you will achieve it all

Sources Of Belief

The source of someone's belief can vary. An extremely weak source would be when someone thinks that they simply "deserve" something, without any other source corroborating why this proclaimed entitlement to the achievement of a goal is a valid expectation. Similarly, wishful thinking is a weak source. When belief is based on experience, obtained in successful comparable previous cases, it has a very strong source. Similarly, when belief is based on goal setting and strong actions to achieve those goals, it has a strong basis. In this way, belief based on a weak source may easily lead to unrealistic expectations of achieving a goal, whereas a strong source may lead to realistic expectations. The stronger your belief, the higher the expectation that the goal will be achieved; the more certainty (likelihood) is allocated to the realisation of success. In this way, strong beliefs may easily lead to disappointments, when the expectations are not met. Having a strong belief is, however, not necessarily bad, on the contrary, it may only create false expectations when you base a strong belief on a weak source. Belief based on a strong source limits the likelihood of over-estimation.
How strong is your belief? What is the main source for your belief? Is it sufficient, or does it need strengthening?

The source of your belief may be weak or strong
Strengthen your source
Through goal setting and focused actions
And your belief will show you the way to success

Using The Power Of Belief

Belief in one's own success is one of the most, if not the most powerful, drivers behind succeeding in what you set out to achieve. Because it is this belief that keeps supplying energy to follow through on your actions, it is this belief which prevents you from giving up when both your progression is lagging and your goal seems to be unattainable. It is this belief which gets you out of bed early morning to start another day in pursuit of your life's goals, it is this belief that inspires others to follow you. When you believe that you will be successful, then you will be successful. So believe in your success and the way to success will follow suit. A strong belief in achievement of a goal sets your mind into overdrive. Your mind (conscious and subconscious) will try to find ways to achieve this goal.

Talk and walk in a way that shows your belief in your own success. Dress in a way that shows you believe in your own success. Show a positive posture and radiate the belief in one's own success. Be enthusiastic when you talk about your future success. Radiate confidence that success is on its way to you, even if you don't see yet how it is going to work out. Feel your success with your heart; be convinced that success will be yours. Then success will come to you, because your belief in your success creates a solid foundation for achieving all your goals.

Do you believe in your own success? Do your talk, posture, dress and the feelings in your heart reflect that belief?

It is this belief that put the first man on the moon in 1969. It is this belief that brought us the Internet. It is this belief that gave us cures for serious diseases. It is this belief that resulted in Skyscrapers. It is this belief that created the sunflower painting. It is this belief that gave us the IPod and the IPhone. It is this belief that built the Great Wall in China. It is this belief that gave us the Harry Potter series of books. It is this belief that resulted in human rights equality. It is this belief that gave Greenpeace its power. It is this belief that will enable you to realise your life's dreams.

But disbelieve, and success will not come. When you believe that you will fail, you will fail. When you half-heartedly believe in the achievement of your goals, you will probably fail. When your attitude is "I will give it a try but it probably won't work anyway", then you are setting yourself up for falling short on your goal's achievement. When you don't even give it a try, because you believe that you will not succeed, you have already failed (Category I). Disbelief is negativity and will attract ways to prove that a goal can't be achieved. It is like a self-fulfilling prophecy. Your subconscious mind starts generating ideas and thoughts supporting failure. These result in actions, which are insufficient for achieving your goal. Because your actions fall short, your conscious mind is strengthened in its view that you are going to fail. Your subconscious mind picks up these signals, and so the downward spiral continues till you cease all action to achieve your goal.

Giving up because of disbelief is one of the most common causes for lack of success.
Are you believing or disbelieving in yourself?

Because believing takes place in your own mind, you are your own worst enemy when it comes to thinking of success. Many of the people in category I can't imagine themselves achieving big successes and doing big things such as improving the lives of many other people. They might think that you need a lot of money, high intellect, university degrees, a good neighbourhood or a different skin colour to be successful. But none of these are true. These are self-created limitations, which have no place in anyone's mind. Because the mind is fully under your own control, anyone can believe in his or her own success. Anyone can imagine and visualise himself or herself as super successful, living the life of their dreams. It is the greatness of your thinking which determines the greatness of your success. So find a big goal, one that you are passionate about, and trigger your self-improvement programme in becoming the person who achieves their goals.
How is your thinking? What is your belief? Are you thinking of big successes, or does your belief keep you captured in Category I?

You are what you think you are. Think that you are a successful person, and you become successful. However, too many people don't give themselves enough credit that they can be a successful person, hence they limit their thinking about their success chances. They think too little of themselves and leave a vast potential, which is within each person, unclaimed. You can use the limitless creativity of your mind to create the biggest success visions for yourself, or you can use the limitless creativity of your mind to develop the worst failures for yourself.
How are you using the limitless creativity of your mind?

What you think of yourself directly influences the way you carry yourself. The way you carry yourself is visible to everyone; you can't hide it. Carry an aura of a successful person, and other people will treat you with the respect for a successful person. On top of that, dressing like a successful person, walking the stride of a successful person, holding your head high, looking other people in the eye, and giving a firm handshake, all support your thinking of success. Carry an aura that you are a failure, and other people will strengthen those feelings. When you dress sloppily, have your head ducked between slumped shoulders, avoid the looks of other people and give weak handshakes, other people pick up those signals and draw their own conclusions. Opportunities for success will unlikely come your way.

How do you carry yourself? How do other people treat you?

Whatever goal you set out, you need to believe that it can be done. This belief sets the conscious and subconscious mind in motion to find ways to realise your belief. You have a mind, it is for you to use and maximise its output. Develop strong beliefs in your successes and have your mind figure out ways to achieving your goals. Your mind will work hard and will not disappoint you. On the other hand, when you have a conviction that you will fail to achieve your goal, your mind will also work hard not to disappoint your expectations. Your mind will prove to you why you will fail. *What do you believe? Is your mind working hard to prove that you will succeed or fail?*

Harness the power of your belief
Believe in success and you will succeed
As your conscious and subconscious mind
Will find ways to realise your belief
You are what you think you are
When you believe you are successful, you will be successful

Using The Law Of Attraction

Popular expressions are: "you are what you think about all day" and "as within, so without". These are rooted in the law of attraction, the law of cause and effect. It is this law of attraction that causes you to attract whatever you focus your energy on. If you believe in (and thus focus your mind on) success, then you will be successful. If you focus your mind on what you don't want (disbelief; failure; non-success), you are unintentionally drawing that into your life. For example, if you constantly think about how difficult it is to achieve a certain goal, you'll actually draw those difficulties and hurdles towards your goal into your life. Instead, when you focus your mind on a smooth progression towards your goals, you intentionally attract situations that enable you to progress towards your goals. It goes without saying that if you focus your attention on achieving a goal and not only believing that you can do it, but that you already have done it, you can achieve virtually any goal you set your mind to. The law of attraction works neutrally, that means in positive as well as negative ways, whether you believe in this law or not. Using the law of attraction to your own benefit means thinking only positive thoughts that help you achieve your life's goals. So believe in your own success towards achieving your goals, and you will be successful. Negative thoughts of failure, doubt and disbelief always bring about negative actions, which in turn result in shortfalls of achieving the goals, and thus non-success.

Success, wealth, good relationships and health do not just drop in your lap by mere wishing to have them. Intentionally harnessing the power of the law of attraction, focussing the law of attraction on what you want to get from life, will give you to what you desire.
Are you already using the law of attraction? Are you using it to its fullest?

Think failure and you will fail
Think success and you will succeed
Consciously use the law of attraction
By thinking positively about your goal achievement
And you will achieve your goals

Strengthening Your Belief

So how do you eliminate disbelief and strengthen belief in your own success? This is possible through a disciplined, focused and trained mind. Consider the following guidance for seizing control over your mind and for changing your mind from a state of disbelief to a state of belief in success:

- Accept that there are certain external circumstances and events over which you have no control (Karma or Fate). They come into your life, whether you want them to or not, and influence your success (goal achievement) in a positive or negative way. Stop resisting things that you can't change on your path to success. Accept them, work with them or find a way around them. Don't let such events rattle you into disbelief. There is a Universal reason why these events come into your life, even when you can't see why that is the case at the moment they arise. Keep believing in your success, and hindsight will show you why these events had to cross your path, and how they steered you on your route to success.

- Don't listen to the disbelief of other people. Other people may try to convince you why you won't be able to achieve your goals. They will bring forward arguments and reasons why you should give up. They tell you "it can't be done" and that you will fail. Listen to them to identify any points that you may need to consider on your path towards your goal. They may highlight good topics for you to address while you strive for a certain goal. Filter out those topics from all the disbelief that they are trying to pass on to you. Then leave it at that and don't let them convince you of their disbelief. Because you have something that they don't have: belief. Don't let them take away your belief when your heart, your gut, your mind, tell you that it can be done, that you will be successful in achieving your goal. Keep an unwavering faith in your success.

- Be grateful: every day express gratitude and be thankful for every progression, however small, towards your goals. Be thankful to people who support you on your way to goal achievement. Deliberately express your gratitude to those people. Say "Thank You" out loud and mean it. Carry gratitude in your thoughts, and say "Thank You" in your mind for each and every progression towards your goals. Acknowledge gratitude for small progression as well as large progression towards your goals. Show gratitude not only in words but also through your actions. Gratitude is important because of the law of attraction. Gratitude means that your mind is thankful for what you have received, and this will bring more of the good stuff to you. The opposite of gratitude is ungratefulness, and when your mind is filled with this, more things will come into your life with which you will be ungrateful.

- Meditate: every day set aside time to seek silence and become one with your goals. Meditation brings peace of mind and allows your mind to focus. Use meditation to strengthen your belief by letting your mind come up with ways to be successful, in ways to achieve your goals. Put your meditative mind to the task of finding ways to navigate around any obstacles on your path to success. Before you go to sleep, let your conscious mind ask your subconscious mind to find ways to increase your success, and your subconscious mind will mull over the topic and reveal its answer in the morning. Develop positive affirmations that strengthen your bond with your goals, and make you believe that you already achieved your goals. Through meditation, set your mind to a condition in which your mind believes that success is possible, as a matter of fact that you already are successful in achieving your goal within the realm of your mind.

- Eliminate self-limiting behaviours and beliefs, as fears and limitations only exist in your mind. When you limit yourself through anxious behaviour such as fear for failure, for loss of face, for being ridiculed for your big goals, for losing friends because they don't believe in you, for set-backs, for what other people might think, for hardship and hard work, you never get anywhere. Fear and other self-limiting beliefs block you on your path to success; they might even prevent you from taking your first step on this path. Sure, some of these things are likely to happen. You are likely to experience setbacks, you likely need to work hard, other people will disbelieve, and they will rattle at your own belief in success. And through the law of attraction, your fear for these things will exactly attract these events and circumstances, because that is what you are thinking about. There is no risk-free life, and without you taking risks, no rewards come your way either. So eliminate those fears and replace them with belief. A belief that at the time that such events and circumstances do happen, you will find a solution for them. A belief that you will be successful in achieving your goal, whatever gets thrown at you while on the pathway to your life's dream. A belief that you have the right goals, for the right reasons and that fears are only a self-created limitation, which may never materialise.

- Think about what you want; don't think about what you don't want. Think about being successful in achieving your goals. Think about successfully overcoming any hurdles on your way to your goals. Think about a smooth path towards goal achievement. Think about having a strong belief in your own success. Think about your victories in your progression towards your goals. Think about how happy you will be when achieving your goals. Don't think about failure. Don't doubt achieving your goals. Don't think about giving up when hurdles cross your path. Don't think about disbelief expressed by other people. Don't think about all the things that could go wrong. Don't think about postponing your first step towards your new goals.

- Use visualisation to strengthen your belief in the achievement of your goals. Bring to your mind the pictures of how it will be when you have achieved your goals. Create those pictures in vivid colours and feel the feelings to accompany the visualisation of having achieved your goals. Believe that you already have achieved your goals, and in your mind create the environment, circumstances and conditions, which exist when you achieve your goals. See those pictures in your mind, hear those sounds in your mind, feel the feeling of achievement, feel your excitement, feel the rush of success, see yourself celebrating your goal achievement. In your mind, shape your world to match your successes, generating pictures of you doing exactly what you set out to do.

- Harbour only positive thoughts about success; observe negative thoughts when they arise, but don't give them attention and eliminate them immediately. Keep your mind focused on the strength of your belief. When your mind is full of strong belief, there is no room for doubts and thoughts of failure to enter and linger on your mind. Sure, doubts about goal achievement, failure to overcome hurdles and thoughts of disbelief will regularly occur. After all, we think many thoughts each day, and positive and negative external events will influence your thinking patterns. But don't give these negative thoughts room to grow. Observe them coming into your mind, but immediately discard them, based on your self-awareness that such doubts will not help you to get from life what you want. As such thoughts do not provide an added value contribution to your goal achievement, they have no place in your mind and no role to play towards your goal achievement.

- Focus on all successes in your life and think of the ways of becoming even more successful. Analyse your past and present successes, and determine what made you so successful in achieving your goals. Think back about what made you start your quest to attain a difficult goal. Reflect on how you were able to overcome even the most difficult hurdles on your path to your goal achievement. Derive confidence and self-belief from the fact that you were victorious before, despite difficult or adverse circumstances. Keep your mind lingering on your successes and project those successes forward to your present goals. Never doubt yourself or dramatize challenges from the past. What can you do to become even more successful? Think about that every day, and take action every day.

- Look for positive aspects in each event, even when at first glance your mind interprets it as a negative event. As you are an integrated part of an ever developing and changing society, it is highly likely that you have a high interdependence on other people. As a result of this interdependence and today's high complexity of the society in which we all live, unexpected events will enter your life, influencing your goal achievement. In nature these events are neutral; they are not good or bad for your success. It is your thinking which labels them as good or bad for your goal achievement. But be careful with this labelling. Diligently analyse each event and don't jump to conclusions, particularly for negative events. There is always a reason why something happens to you. This Universe is a friendly Universe and always gives you what is best for you, even when at first glance it might not seem this way. This concept might be difficult to understand, but think about it. Think back to negative events blocking your way to goal achievement and then contemplate how these events gave you a different twist on your pathway, and ultimately something else good came out of these events. When your time horizon for such analysis is long enough, you will always be able to identify why negative events crossed your path, because of the necessary twist that you needed in order to succeed towards your goals. Because of the interdependence of your life on the lives of other people, the road to successful goal achievement is not always the shortest road. The shortest and most direct road may lead to failure, as life will have built in detours for specific reasons. So don't be too fast in jumping to conclusions regarding negative events. Look for the positive aspects and your belief in goal achievement will remain strong.

- Reflect on yourself: consciously observe your own thoughts and feelings that may weaken your belief in success. Be aware of what you are thinking, particularly when thoughts enter your mind making you doubt your own success or giving you feelings of failure. Keep a wiretap on your conscious mind, and let the alarm bells go off when you notice thoughts, which do not help you in achieving your goals. When some form of disbelief enters your mind, take immediate corrective action. Analyse the causes of those thoughts of disbelief and take action to remove them, so that your mind can settle in the thoughts of belief again. Argue with yourself why those weakening thoughts should be abandoned, why they should not deserve any attention from your mind.

- Don't be concerned with judgment of others, when other people express their disbelief and state that you can't achieve your goal. Other people may be jealous of your goal, other people may fail to see how you will get it done, other people may be ignorant of your skills, determination and passion for your goal, other people may have tried and failed themselves, other people may not wish you success, other people may lack your vision, other people may have given up hope on improving their life, other people may not have read this book. There are many reasons why other people will try to convince you not to pursue your goals. But their disbelief has no role to play in your life. Your own belief that you have the right goals for the right reasons is the only matter that counts.

- Don't measure yourself against others: think about your own dream, follow your own heart and passions. Your belief needs to come from you yourself. You need to believe that you will be successful because of what you bring to the table for achieving your goals. Your goals are based on your desires, on your passion, and on your dream for how your life should look. Other people follow their own dreams, and the Universe will give them what is best for them. Measuring yourself against the failures of other people won't get you anywhere either. Other people's disbelief has no place in your mind. Of course you can learn from the mistakes that other people have made, and draw the positive lessons from their unsuccessful efforts, but don't let this rattle your own belief. Actually, it should strengthen your belief that you do things your own way, at your own pace, for your own goals, and that you will be successful, because you are different from all the others who have failed. Similarly, be careful with comparing yourself to other people that were already successful. Sure, learn what worked well for them, analyse the basis of their success and apply success-generating principles also to the achievement of your own goals. But don't measure yourself against their success, because their circumstances may have been different, their goals may have been different, their efforts may have been different, etc. Let their success inspire you and strengthen your belief that it can be done, but don't compare the details of your goals and progress.

How do you strengthen your belief in your success?

Strengthen your belief in success
Accept that there are certain events over which you have no control
Don't listen to the disbelief of other people
Each day express gratitude for each progression towards your goals
Meditate to focus your mind on success
Eliminate self-limiting behaviours and beliefs
Think about what you want; don't think about what you don't want
Use visualisation in the achievement of your goals
Discard negative thoughts when they arise
Focus on all past and present success in your life
Think of ways to become even more successful
Look for positive aspects in each negative event
Reflect on yourself and what you are thinking
Don't be concerned with judgment of others
Don't measure yourself against others

Controlling Your Mind

There are 24 hours in a day, and although your subconscious mind works 24/7, your conscious mind does not. You need your conscious mind to reprogram your subconscious mind. Each awaking day you have a continuous flow of many different thoughts, sometimes of longer duration, sometimes just popping in and out of your mind. Mind control makes it possible for you to channel the thoughts that go through your mind and concentrate on those thoughts that help you achieve your goals in life. Since negative thoughts don't provide a contribution to reach your life's goals, you can observe them coming into existence in your mind, and subsequently immediately discard them. This creates space in your mind that you can keep filled with positive thoughts, belief in your success and achievement of your goals. When your mind is full of positive success thoughts, there is no space for negative failure thoughts to arise and linger.

It is your belief, your faith, which makes you succeed. Let the thought "I am successful" be your dominant thought. Because the mind will find ways to satisfy your dominant thoughts: it searches for ways to make you successful. It will develop action plans to help you progress towards your goals. The Universe picks up on your dominant thought and generates circumstances and conditions, which provide opportunities to enable your success.

You already possess all the power to be successful within you, you just need to unlock it and use it. Your mind is creative, and has the capacity to create yourself as well as your environment. The mind can conceive anything that you want, but it is your responsibility to steer your mind in the direction of your goals and success. For this you need to control your mind, and make sure it focuses on you progressing through life. Your mind can overcome any obstacle that comes in your way to success. The power of your mind is phenomenal, but you need to control and direct it to ensure that it works for your benefit. Let it run wild and it may likely work to your detriment. The choice is really yours.
Are you already harnessing the power of your mind?

Your thinking creates your environment. Think successes and goal achievement, and you will eventually live in an environment full of success. The environment around you is a reflection of the way you think about your life. You have to think about what you want and that you can have what you want, irrespective of your current circumstances. Keep success in mind, even when you experience setbacks. Keep wealth in mind, even when you are poor. Keep health in mind, even when you are ill. Keep peace and tranquillity in mind, even when you are in a hostile environment. Keep a loving relationship in mind, even when you are in a divorce.

Think as a person in Category I, and you will live in an environment that shows non-success. Your house, your furniture, your car, your clothing, your food, your neighbourhood, your social relationships and your job will all reflect that you have given up on any goals in life, without even having put in the efforts in trying first. Think as a person in Category III, and you will live in an environment that shows success. Your house, your furniture, your car, your clothing, your food, your neighbourhood, your social relationships and your job will all reflect that you are successful in life and that you are living your passion. This is why Category I and III people never live in the same neighbourhood, their children go to different schools, their cars are different, their houses are different, they dress differently, their vacations take them to different destinations, etc.

Is your environment reflecting category I? Are you satisfied with that, or do you want the same as the people in the category III? Are you taking "inside" actions to change your "outside" conditions?

Your mind is creative. This means that your mind creates your external conditions relating to your environment and all the experiences in your life. The links between those external conditions and your mind are your perpetual and prevailing thoughts. This means that the secret to all your success and achievement lie in the way you think. It is your prevailing and persistent thoughts on any subject that bring that subject into reality in your external conditions. Since your mind is creative and there are no limitations to this creativity, you can achieve and be successful in virtually anything you want. What it needs is consistent and unwavering thinking about those conditions, and you will realise them. When you are thinking one goal this week, another goal next week, and in the third week something new again, you are not committing yourself enough to one important goal. It is like your mind is a vessel that is steered by the wind blowing from different directions. With changing winds (your thinking), you won't get anywhere. In order to improve your current conditions, you will need to have a destination. Without a destination, your vessel doesn't know where to go, and you will stay where you are. You need to decide on your destination.

What destination are you providing to your vessel? Are you setting direction with destination Category III environment? Or are you waiting your whole life without going anywhere, only dreaming about the far away destinations?

Mere dreaming does not make you change your external environment. You need consistent and unwavering thinking about the external conditions to realise them. Your mind initiates actions for topics that are persistently and dominantly present in your thoughts. The reason is that your mind needs time to develop action plans to turn your thinking into external conditions. Actions plans need execution and traction before your external conditions

start changing. You need to prepare yourself for the changes and develop opportunities to cement those desired changes. Your today's external conditions are the result of how you have been thinking in the past years. Change your thinking to change your external conditions. Your persistent thoughts are the causes, and your external conditions are the mere effects.
Are you presently in Category I? Is it correct that your predominant thinking was like a Category I person in the last years?
Are you presently in category II? Is it correct that you were thinking like a Category III person for a long time, but that your prevailing thoughts changed to Category II?
Are you presently in category III? Is it correct that your predominant thinking was like a Category III person in the last years?

When you want to exploit the power of your creative mind, you need to control your mind. You need to change simple thinking, dreaming and chaotic and unfocused thoughts, into directed, concentrated, methodical, positive, conscious and productive thinking.
How are the thoughts in your mind? Are they many different thoughts, or do the majority of your daily thoughts focus on one and the same topic?

Are your thousands of thoughts day after day linked to every little detail that happens in your life? From not wanting to get up when the alarm buzzes in the morning, getting annoyed when your morning paper did not arrive, thinking howcome the person in front of you in the traffic jam is able to afford that expensive car, trying ways to stretch your lunch break, wondering when you will find time to work in the garden, what is on television tonight, till what clothes to wear the next day shortly before you fall asleep. Do these thoughts repeat day after day? Then you are likely in Category I, and your life is not really progressing. You seem to be stuck in the same rut, without seeing a way out?

On the other hand, when your mind and thoughts are focused, the majority of your daily thoughts revolve around one big topic. It could be your business, it could be the big project that you are working on, it could be your upcoming exam, or any other main subject that is driving you in your daily activities towards an overarching goal. When your alarm buzzes in the morning, you think about the objectives for the day, and how you will realise those, when your morning paper does not arrive you take the extra time to be early in the office, in the traffic jam you mentally prepare yourself for the morning meeting in the office or with a customer, you eat at your desk while you continue to write an important report, you have allotted fixed time for your family and for working in the garden, you have no time to watch television at night because you are taking an evening course, before falling asleep you go over your successes during the day and think about ways of how you can be even more successful the next day. Do these thoughts repeat day after day? Then you are likely in Category II or III, and your life is progressing towards one big goal. When this one big goal is maintaining status quo of your external conditions and your life, you are in Category II. Your thinking is focused, but the focus is on maintaining what you have. When your thinking is progressive, and you shift from one big goal to an even bigger goal, you are in Category III.

You can control what you are thinking about the whole day. You can steer your thoughts. You have the full power to make your thoughts clear, focused, persistent. It is really up to you to harness this power of controlling your mind. When your current external conditions reflect a Category I, persistent thinking like a Category III person, will change those external conditions. It is only a matter of time till they match your thinking, and you find yourself in a Category III environment. You can create all the things and success that you desire. Controlling your thinking might not be so easy when you are not used to this. The beauty is that anyone can learn it. It needs persistent practice, just like when you want to grow your muscles: endurance and practice will get you there.

The conscious mind only works while you are awake. In contrast, your subconscious mind never stops working. It works while you are sleeping and it works while your conscious mind is inactive. Your subconscious mind mainly regulates your breath, your heartbeat, and your other bodily functions. It is also a potential source for thought. But this source needs to be activated. While your conscious mind will almost automatically generate many thoughts each day, your subconscious mind must be triggered into thinking. Your subconscious mind is susceptible to the will of the conscious mind: it accepts anything from the conscious mind as true. The will of the conscious mind is chiselled in the subconscious mind by the focused and persistent thoughts. For anything that gets impressed in the subconscious mind, this mind believes it as true and will find ways to support this truth. When your persistent thoughts are those of failure, that you don't have what it takes to become successful, your subconscious mind thinks of ways to make you fail. It will come up with even more excuses why you won't be able to become successful. It will influence your daily actions and your conscious thought patterns to achieve a result of failure. On the other hand, when you impress success on your subconscious mind, this mind sees it as true that you are successful, and thinks of more ways to support your success. It will influence your daily actions and your conscious thoughts to achieve a result of success.

Because the subconscious mind won't argue, you can ask anything from it. When what you're asking is uncontrolled, you might get the following results. If you have thousands of different thoughts in your conscious mind, day after day, all about the daily trivial events, without any pattern or persistence to some sort of overarching and progressive future goal, your subconscious mind remains non-activated and unnoticed in the shadows of your conscious mind. You may now and then get a glimpse of its existence, but your subconscious mind probably only supports your conscious mind with worrying, fears, agitations, distress, angst and anxiety. When you ask for negativity, the subconscious mind assists to generate negativity. Impress failure on the subconscious mind, and it thinks of ways to support your failure. When you ask for success, the subconscious mind finds ways to make you successful. When you ask your subconscious mind to resolve a specific problem for you, it tries to find solutions for your problem. When you ask your subconscious mind to help you overcome certain challenges, it provides assistance to overcome those challenges. It generates solutions, ideas, actions that address the specific problem that has been brought to its attention. But think that a problem cannot be overcome, and it finds ways to support that thesis. So be careful and specific what you imprint on and ask from your subconscious mind.
How does this work in your mind? Do you harness the enormous power of your subconscious mind? Are you directing what goes into your subconscious mind (and thus what comes out), or are you passively accepting what comes out without directing its focus?

Control your minds
Let your conscious mind reprogram your subconscious mind
Direct what goes into both your minds
Don't let any thoughts of failure enter your minds
Focus your minds on your goals and success
Let your subconscious mind work out solutions for you

STEP 4

TAKING CONSISTENT AND FOCUSED ACTIONS

Acting In The Here And Now

You can only be successful when you take action, otherwise your dream will always stay a dream. The doers of this world become successful. Only thinking and talking about doing will not make you successful: you have to act. Regardless of how good your idea is, if you don't act, it will always stay an idea. Only actions can turn an idea into a pot of gold.

But when do you start acting on a goal or idea? What is the appropriate timing? Do you start acting when the conditions and circumstances are ideal, and there are no risks involved, no downsides anymore? Yes, this would be ideal, but since this is unlikely to happen, you should not wait for the perfect opportunity to come your way, as it does not exist. In each and every situation you can expect drawbacks and reasons why not to start acting right this instance. If you wait for that perfect opportunity you will never start. This is valid for every person looking for success, not just you. But the successful people have the courage to make a start in uncertain conditions without knowing for certain what the outcome will be. Many people, especially those in Category I, let their fears freeze them from taking action. They start thinking what if I fail to obtain the finances for my business, what if I can't attract sufficient customers, what if my product fails, what if the competition is too strong, what if nobody buys my product, etc. Their negative thinking results in fear for failure, which results in non-action. To play it "safe" they don't take any actions and continue a dull life. But without risks there are no rewards. You need to take risks if you want to be rewarded in the achievement of your goal. They want to wait till they have reduced all uncertainties and risks to zero. They wait till they have obtained their finances, till their product is perfect, till they have many customers, till there is no competition. And you know what? That situation never arises if you don't first start. Thus they never take that first step and keep postponing their start to success indefinitely. On the other hand, successful people know how to handle uncertainty and risks. They overcome their fears for failure and dare to take a risk, as the big prize of success oftentimes is a manifold of the size of the risks that they take. They take the first step and continue to learn how to handle risks and uncertainties as they move forward on the pathway to success. Successful people understand that the starting situation is never ideal, and that there are going to be difficulties, obstacles and setbacks in the future. But they do not let them influence their decision to make this start. Successful people

don't eliminate all problems and difficulties before they start, rather they have confidence that they will be able to overcome these difficulties and problems when they arise.
Are you playing it safe, and postpone acting on your dreams?

When an opportunity arises, which brings you closer to your goal, and you feel yourself drawn to it, take it. Each journey to success starts with a single first step. When this first step brings you closer to your goal, take that first step. Only by taking actions can you advance your life. You need to start now, today. Start with small things and learn as you go along. Your learning curve increases exponentially once you start doing. Nothing can beat the practical experience of having done something. It does not matter what you know when you start on the pathway to your goal, rather your learning and self-improvement capability is what counts. Along the way your confidence and personality grow and your goals will grow with you. But you need to take that first step. After you have taken the first step and you see that the world has not collapsed on you, your self-confidence will grow. This motivates for more action, increasing your belief and trust in yourself. You become more assertive and firm with your goal, strengthening your resolve and positive outlook. You develop your character as you take more steps towards success. Those that wait, postpone, delay, procrastinate and stall, increase their fears, incur negative psychological effects and increase the likelihood that they will never take that first step. Waiting and postponing actions and decisions is easy. Because it is easy, it won't lead you anywhere. You stay where you are, without advancing your life.
Do you take the easy way, or do you have the courage to make today the first day of your new life?

You can't act in the past, as the past has already ended. You can't act in the future, because the future still needs to begin. You must act in the here and now, at this moment in time. Don't wait with actions till the circumstances are perfect, because they never will be. If you don't like the circumstances that you are in now, start taking action to change those circumstances to what you want them to be. Accept your present external conditions as they are, because they are a result of your past investments. Then work within your present conditions as a basis from where you catapult yourself to a better environment, one that reflects your desires and dreams. Start taking actions to progress towards your goal now, as this is the only way you can start. Don't put things off which can be done today, as you only get from where you are to where you want to be by taking action. The sooner you take action the sooner you arrive at your destination. If you are running a marathon, the only way to cover the 42.2 kilometers is to do it step by step, all 40'000 of them. It is the same with the pathway to your goal. You need to take action after action, day after day, to achieve your goal.

Don't wait for the right time, right circumstances before you act
These will never occur
Have the courage to make a start in uncertain conditions
Regardless of how good your idea is, if you don't act
It will always stay an idea
Only actions can turn an idea into a pot of gold
Start your action to success now

Making A Detailed Action Plan

There comes a time in your life when you need to set priorities and determine what is really important to you. If you have a dream worthwhile achieving, you must take action to turn your goal into reality. You need to be serious about the planning and your intentions to take the required actions if you want to achieve your goals. If you don't make an action plan, you are leaving your goal's progression to chance and to the influx of uncoordinated ideas for actions. Without serious planning, you don't know for certain that your actions will take you where you want to go. Serious action planning accelerates your progress and strengthens the results.
How serious is your action planning? Is it just in your head, or is it documented?

How to set up an action plan? Start with picturing the end-result. What is your goal, see it in detail, visualise it, see it clearly and transparently. Then start working backwards what steps you need to undertake to achieve this goal. When your goal spans multiple years or even decades, your action plan must also span multiple years or decades. The further away in the future, the rougher and more general your action plan becomes. It is in the nature of time that the more in the future, the more difficult it becomes to exactly predict your status on your goal progression and thus the required actions

needed to keep you advancing. On the other hand, the closer in time (hours, days, weeks, months), the more concrete, detailed and precise your action planning must be. If you are presently a law student at University, your action plan to achieve your goal of partner in a law firm could be as follows: Today: attend law class; Tomorrow: pass an exam at University; Next week: attend career day; Next month: apply for internship at a law firm; Next Quarter: pass an exam at University; Next year: apply at law firm; In 2 years: pass the bar exam; In 5 years: specialise in one area of the law; In 10 years: become partner.
Do you have multi-year action plans for your long-term goals?

Set up a step-by-step plan, write it out, and keep track of your progress. Your detailed plan regulates your progression, gives you direction, prepares you for the actions, focuses your energy and keeps you attached to your goal. So follow it persistently and consistently once you are satisfied with the quality and content of your plan. Be clear on your goal, and create a focused and clear action plan. Without a clear goal, your action plan can't be focused either. Similarly, scattering your efforts over too many goals diffuses your efforts. The components of a good action plan are as follows:

- Establish a clear and transparent goal. You need to know and understand your goal in detail. Make sure that your goal is based on your desires and passions, as these are needed to fuel your actions and keep the energy and enthusiasm.

- Break down your long-term goal into mid-term and short-term goals. Set up timelines and milestones by when you want to have achieved which goal. Make sure that all intermediate goals focus on the ultimate long-term goal.

- Do your research and find out everything you can about the pathway to your long-term goal. What do you need in terms of skills, tools, money, education, experience and equipment? Vague notions and unclear ideas need to be worked out and turned into crystal clear understanding of what it needs to achieve your goals, before setting out on your quest for them.

- Specify the actions required to attain the short-, medium, and long-term goals. Write these actions down in a detailed action plan to serve as your guide for your everyday actions and your preparation for future actions. A structured and precise plan keeps your focus on the goal, provides a means for measuring and correcting progress and gives you the possibility to acclaim intermediate successes. Seeing yourself progress in accordance with your plan will make you feel good and positive, strengthening your determination and persistence to see your actions through till the end.

- Plan for success through education, preparation, training and experience, as part of a self-improvement programme to a successful you.

- Make a daily schedule of your actions, and stick to your schedule. Each day do what you can do to progress towards your goals. Prioritise your actions. During your morning meditation session, prepare yourself for that day's actions and link them to your goals. Let the passion for your goals spur you on, to energetic and enthusiastic action each day.

- Regularly review your detailed action plan to ensure it still realises your dreams and desires. Make adjustments when circumstances change, or planned actions are not effective.

Hoe does your action plan look like? Did you write it out on paper?

Also get excited about the pathway in achieving the goal, the planning thereof, the actions thereof, the execution thereof, etc., not just about the goal itself. Because when the pathway is long, and the goal far ahead, you risk losing your motivation, drive, passion, when you are not enjoying the road itself. Love to get challenged and roll up your sleeves to get actions done every day. Love the overtime or early morning hours, hardship, etc. You need to enjoy the road before you can enjoy reaching the goal. If you don't enjoy the road, you will never achieve the goal. You are likely to give up along the way or not start at all. The only way to enjoy the road is when passion and desires propel you forward. So make sure that your motivation comes from your passion.
Are you excited about the pathway to your goals?

Your detailed action plan does not need to resolve all possible problems before they happen. Until you are really into your activity and executing your action plan, you don't know exactly where the problems will arise

anyway. Society is developing, you are developing, your business/career is progressing and obstacles that you foresaw when you were making your plan might have disappeared altogether by the time you arrive at that point. Or when the obstacles do cross your pathway, you have gained the necessary experience to smoothly handle them. Your detailed action plan needs to have a certain level of flexibility. Don't make it too rigid. You must keep room for detours or opportunities that come your way along the pathway to success. When you take a detour, it does not mean that you give up on your goal; it just means that you take a different pathway.
Are you leaving room for flexibility into your action plans?

Set up a step-by-step action plan
Write it out, and keep track of your progress
Your detailed plan regulates your progression
Gives you direction, prepares you for the actions
Focuses your energy and keeps you attached to your goal
Your detailed plan shouldn't be too rigid
And does not need to resolve all problems before they happen

Taking Action Every Day

Don't you know people who always talk about great ideas, about how they are going to move up in life, about them seizing the next opportunity, but in reality never move an inch from their spot? Talking does not move you forward, doing does. You need to start taking action day after day to make your goal a reality. Procrastination is a goal killer. Delay an action and you will lose valuable time in achieving your goal. The more you postpone, the longer it takes and the more difficult it gets to execute the action later on. So get into action now and do each day what you can do to move you closer to your goals. Unfortunately, it is too easy to go about your day and let the small daily events and disruptions steer you through life. It takes no effort at all to let yourself be submerged in the daily small occurrences and succumb to whatever comes your way. The TV is another goal killer. Get

rid of the TV and procrastination, and consciously steer your life towards your dreams by taking every kind of action it needs, every day, making you progress towards your goals.
What are the goal killers in your life? How can you get rid of them?

You must do each day what you can do that day. You don't need to rush your actions, you don't need to do overtime, or do the work that can be done tomorrow today. It is the efficiency and effectiveness of your actions that count, not the number of hours that you put in. Efficient action means trying to achieve as much as possible with as low as possible effort. Effective actions mean that your actions lead you closer to your goals.
How efficient and effective are your daily actions?

When you lead a balanced life, you have multiple goals and thus multiple actions. Make a schedule for your daily actions and ensure that over time you achieve a balanced progress to your life's goals. If you have the goals of mindfulness, a fit and strong body, a steep career path and a loving relationship with your spouse, family and friends, you have to invest in each of these goals. You need to take action every day to keep yourself progressing in a balanced way. You could wakeup earlier to meditate and do a workout before you rush to the office. After work or in the weekend you need to study in order to progress in your career. You need to be at home to have dinner with the family and spend time with the kids before they go to bed. Being successful does not only mean achieving one goal at a time, but also progressing to and achieving multiple goals at the same time. This is when it becomes hard and your daily actions are in competition with different goals. But when you are passionate about being mindful, when you are passionate about your physical status, when you are passionate about your career and when you are passionate about your family, you are going to have all the energy, willpower and devotion to advance on all fronts.
Are your daily actions spread over multiple goals?

Taking action every day keeps your goal at the forefront of your thoughts. It keeps your focus on the purposeful and sustainable goals in your life. Stop taking action every day, and you won't advance towards your goal, and soon your goal disappears in the fog of your memories. You fall back in the old routines of a dull life. On the other hand, the more steps you take, the easier it is to increase your pace, until finally you are running towards your goal. Keep yourself in action to achieve your goals. Actions increase the level of anticipation of reaching a goal. That is why doing nothing rarely

makes people happy, but being active in the pursuit of a meaningful goal does.
Are you already running?

Talking does not move you forward
Doing does
You need to take action day after day to make your goal a reality
Procrastination is a goal killer
Each day you must do whatever you can do that day
It is the efficiency and effectiveness of your actions that count
Not the number of hours you put in
Taking action every day keeps your goal in your thoughts
It keeps your focus on the purpose of your life

Success Does (Not Necessarily) Need Hard Work

Didn't your parents tell you to work hard in order to have a chance at becoming successful? Don't all books and empirical studies on success say that you need to work hard or the hardest to become successful? Only the person who puts in most hours becomes successful compared to the other people striving for the same success? Well, success does (not necessarily) need hard work.

Sure hard work will be required from time to time, but hard work itself does not make you successful. There are many people who work hard, 6 or 7 days per week in 12-hour shifts, like the diamond miners in South Africa or the crew doing the laundry on board of cruise ships. Do these miners or laundry crews get rich from their hard work? No. So hard work itself is not a determinant for success. Rather, if you get all other factors for success right, you do not need to work hard, and can still be successful!

How can this work? You do not need to overwork to exhaustion to be successful. That is a fairy-tale. You need to do the right things efficiently and apply the Pareto Principle. This principle says that often times you can achieve 80% of the result with only 20% efforts. To get from 80% to 100% of your goal consumes 80% of your efforts. So you need to decide whether 80% of your goal achievement is sufficient, or whether you indeed want and need to go all the way to 100% goal achievement. There may be many situations where 80% goal achievement is sufficient, whereas you can also think about examples where 100% is required. Take the matter of hygiene when you run a restaurant. A goal of 80% hygienic conditions will soon leave you without customers, as they will stay away when food is not fresh or they find things in their food that should not be in it, or when the authorities suspend your business license. Another example is when you are a plumber. Allowing the gas and water tubes to leak 20% of the time would very quickly get you out of business. Liability claims would ruin you. On the other hand, when you set a goal of earning $1 million of income each year, and you achieve $800'000 with only 20% of your efforts, you are probably going to be satisfied with that. Instead of spending 80% of your time and resources to earn another $200'000, it could be much more interesting to spend that 80% on different purposes instead of slaving away to bring in the final 20%. A better alternative might be to set up a second business with new goals or to become a global traveller, simply enjoying life, having all the time and money to do so. When you have the goal to learn a new language or lose 20 pounds of weight, you will surely be very happy when you reach 80% language proficiency or lose 16 pounds. To achieve the remainder of the 20% language fluency or to lose the last 4 pounds might be extremely difficult and take a lot more effort than those first 80%. In these cases, 80% is usually good enough. Oftentimes perfection is not needed, and it is better to complete your project or service when it is good enough, instead of trying to reach perfection at 100%. Perfection at that level might never be reached, at least not in an economical way. So reaching 80% of your goal might actually be good enough to be successful and move on to the next level of bigger goals.

Are you striving for perfection, 100% goal achievement? Is that necessary, or could 80% achievement also be acceptable?

When you are active in the competitive field, then getting better than others can usually only be achieved through hard work, by working harder than others. It is working harder in combination with working smarter than others that will get you ahead of other people, and thus become successful.

This is often your only way to success as you have to become better than others, requiring harder work, longer hours, more overtime, longer study time, more experience, etc. Take the example of a law firm. The higher the number of billable hours, the more chance you have to progress within the hierarchy of the firm. The lawyer with the most billable hours will do best in this extremely competitive environment. Another example is the professions based on pure physical work. Working in the fields, behind the counter of the fast food chain, security at airports, or cleaning hotel rooms. These jobs are easy, thus many people can do them and many people want to do them, resulting in a large supply of workforce. The large supply and thus high competition keeps their salaries low. Many are paid on hourly and quantity wages, so the harder you work, the more hours you make or the more you produce, the more salary you can take home. But you won't get rich from working the many hours.
Are you active in the competitive field? Do you work long hours but don't get anywhere with your life?

On the creative field, this is structurally different. Hard work itself is not a basis for success, because it depends what you are working on. Do you work hard on things in competition with many other people, or do you work hard on something where there is no competition because you are on the creative field? Everybody can work hard, but not everybody can (or wants to) be creative. When you are creative you are developing a product or service that does not yet exist. The people working in the Research & Development departments of companies are a good example, but so are writers, musicians, painters, film directors, dancers and fashion designers. To come back to the example of the lawyers: the top lawyers are creative as well. The same is valid for the top investment bankers, top CEOs, and other top business performers. These people use their mind to create something new. Those thoughts of creation do not require making as many as possible hours each day, seven days a week. Rather, creativity is based on inspiration and thinking out of the box. It is true that each creator is in competition with another creator, but when you compare the number of creators in a field to the number of people who work on an hourly basis competing against each other, there are many less. Because of much less competition in the creative field, it requires less hard work to be successful being creative. Success in creativity mostly depends on how distinctively different your service or product is compared to another creator or previous creations from other people.
Are you already active on the creative field? Do you have a passion that could enable this?

Let me give an example of how in the creative field the Pareto Principle works best, even to extremes. Sometimes it takes a musician only a couple of hours, or even less, to create a new song text and accompanying melody. Still, this new song may be enormously successful and sell millions of times, or even tens of millions of times when you stretch the time period, bringing abundant royalty income and thus wealth to the musician. These are of course extremes, but they do happen and the key point is that on the creative field hard work is not a guarantor for success, but creating something interestingly different and new is. Of course the musician is not without competition either, as many new songs are created each day. The creation of the new songs happens on the creative field, but then the song is moved to the competitive field to get it noticed, to get it marketed and sold, which may require hard work and many efforts. There the song competes with many other new songs, as well as the alternative spending possibilities for the buyers of the songs. If the musician has already achieved success and fame, then the mere publishing of the song can already be sufficient to generate significant cash flow, and no hard work to get it noticed, marketed and sold is necessary. The new song automatically sells because of the good reputation of the musician. This is the ultimate and most extreme situation where little work is needed but the creative product still becomes extremely successful in generating cash flow and thus wealth. Isn't this the ultimate dream for success? It doesn't get much bigger than this, and you should milk it when you are at that stage in your life. There are many real life examples of people that have accomplished this such as JK Rowling, Mick Jagger, Steve Jobs and Jeff Koons. But you should not forget that each of these people had to work hard and go through tough times before they reached this level of fame and success.

To link this topic back to an earlier chapter, wealth accumulation only happens when your service or product adds some sort of value to the buyer, and the buyer is willing to pay a cash premium. When you are active on the competitive field it is extremely difficult or almost impossible to add value to your service, as the activity in which you are engaged is usually limited- to non-adding value. A customer will not pay more for a product because it is you standing behind the counter of the supermarket, fast food chain or music store. Therefore, creating added value for a customer happens mostly in the creative field. That is why the creative professions can often times command high salaries. There is limited competition being a creator, and the accumulation of cash premiums paid by the customers warrants a high income for the creator. This gets even better when you are the creator of an

added value service or product in your own company, when it is you who controls and acquires all cash premiums. That is the only way to acquire significant wealth. To many people wealth symbolises success, so you can say, this is how you can become super successful. Generally speaking, a person in Category I is active in the competitive field, whereas a person in category III is active in the creative field.
Do you have a goal to become super successful and accumulate wealth? In which playing field are you active? Do you need to switch field?

Success does (not necessarily) need hard work
You need to work smart: efficient and effective
Use the Pareto Principle, instead of perfection
In the competitive field success is achieved by working harder
In the creative field this is structurally different
As you can work on something without competition
This is the only way to become super successful and wealthy

The Ethical Side Of Actions

You can get addicted to the feelings of success, which may result in you always wanting to win, or succeed, in what you are doing. When you put success, the achievement of your goals, above everything else, including the ethics of your life and profession, you go overboard. You put yourself in a situation, which is not sustainable. You will not be able to sustain success when you are willing to attain this at all cost. Like with everything in life, also success has an ethical side. Being successful at the cost of other people, through illegal means, through cheating, violence, criminal activities or fraud, will not lead to happiness. We all strive towards success with the underlying goal of becoming happy. Goals attained by unethical means will not lead to long-lasting happiness, because the external environment will put energy in undoing the unethical behaviour and in the redistribution of gains obtained through this behaviour. For example, a person may have the goal of getting rich, in an easy and quick way. They may rob a bank, cheat investors through a Ponzi scheme, use doping to win the race or steal intellectual property from other people. Such a person may indeed achieve their goal, and become successful, however, it is very unlikely that this goal achievement can be maintained for a long time. It is very likely that the negative consequences (fear for being caught, negative energy which has to be put in to keep the scheme hidden, risk of spending the money from the bank robbery) of the unethical behaviour lead to such emotional pressures that such a person is not able to enjoy their success. The negative consequences of the unethical behaviour are likely to overshadow the positive impact from achieving the goal.

What is the ethical side of your goal achievement and your actions? Are you crossing the line?

Your actions to realise your dream should not be at the cost of realisation of the dreams of other people. In such case your realisation would be in direct competition with the efforts of other people, and two people would be fighting over the same resource. When this fighting over the same resource takes place with unethical means, the rules of the success game are broken, and societal forces will be provoked to reverse these actions. In achieving your own goal, you don't need to take away things from other people. Not their money, not their dignity, not their belief, not their humanity, not their trust, etc. There is an abundance of everything in this Universe, and your success will only feel like a success when this is achieved in an ethical manner.

Are you taking away things from other people in order to achieve your goal?

Success is bound by rules of Ethics
In achieving successful goal achievement
Don't take away things from other people
Give added value to other people

Self-Investment For Self-Improvement

You must be willing to take chances to try out something new. You only move forward when you get out of your comfort zone and dare to take risks. You are going to be left behind when you stick to old habits and processes. The world around you is rapidly evolving and change is permanent and continually accelerating. You have to be open to new experiences, new procedures, and new ways of doing things; otherwise you won't progress in your life. Your environment will continue to develop, while you linger in a standstill and get left behind. A successful person develops himself faster than his environment is evolving. A super successful person develops himself much faster than his environment is progressing. He is ahead of the pack and leads and steers the development of the environment. It is he who sets the direction and pace for the advancement of many millions of other people. Think about Bill Gates, Henry Ford, Thomas Cook, Leonardo Da Vinci, and the other great entrepreneurs and original creative thinkers.

You need to remain open to new ideas otherwise you won't develop yourself. Have an open mind for new information and opportunities to develop yourself. Never assume that you already know everything there is to know, as there are always different perspectives, new approaches and developing circumstances.
Are you open to new ideas? Do you have an open mind?

Once you set a goal, you need to do your research and find out everything you can about the pathway to your goal. Visualising your goal and deeply understanding what you will be like when you achieve your goal is getting to know the person you will become in the future. The traits of your future self do not depend on what you do once you achieved your goal, but rather on your investment today. You need to invest in yourself today to become that future successful you. What do you need in terms of skills, tools, money, education, experience and equipment? You must embark on a self-improvement programme. You must invest in yourself. Investing in yourself means planning for success through education, preparation, training and experience. You might have to learn new skills, get new experience, expand your mind through education or train your body.
Do you know which self-investment is needed to get you to success? Are you willing to embark on a self-improvement programme?

Investing in yourself does not necessarily require a lot of money. There is so much information freely available on the Internet, and millions of books are published each year, accessible through public libraries. Read one stimulating book every two months. Books provide a number of advantages: you can learn from mistakes of other people, so that you avoid making that mistake yourself; they expedite your learning process; they give you ideas to create new opportunities; they expand your knowledge; they give you multiple perspectives; they are flexible in that you can learn when you have time for it. Reading inspirational books is one of the best investments for self-improvement and generating new ideas.

Investing in yourself does require time. You need to self-invest by making time available. That requires commitment and willpower. Isn't it much easier to spend the evening zapping the TV channels instead of taking a book in your hands? You can easily find time by replacing those activities (like watching TV) that do not contribute to your goal achievement, with activities that do (like reading books). It is all a matter of setting the right priorities.
Do you make sufficient time and money available for your self-improvement programme?

The world is continually progressing and developing
You can only be successful when you progress as well
Invest in your self-improvement, and become a better you
Get the required education, experience, knowledge and training
Read one inspirational book every two months
Give this priority over activities that don't help you advance

Managing Other People To Your Success

Success rarely comes without the involvement of other people, whatever business you are in. Your skills in managing other people are therefore extremely relevant to your success. Key to your success is getting the cooperation of other people. They might be your subordinates, your suppliers, your boss, your peers, and most importantly your (internal or external) customers. Ultimately your customers provide the benchmark for your success. Do they buy your service or product, and are they willing to pay a monetary premium for the added value? From whatever perspective you look at your success: it depends on the free and willing cooperation of other people.
Have you identified the key stakeholders and contributors to your success?

The following are a number of key principles, which help you secure the cooperation of other people on the pathway to your goals:

- You have limited capacity yourself: you have to delegate tasks to other people, such as subordinates and suppliers. Delegation only works when the other people understand your goals, not just their own role, but their role in harmony with your goals. You have a grand vision of a purposeful goal in your mind. You are passionate about your goal, and go to lengths to achieve your goal. Put your grand vision in the heads of the people supporting you; make them share your enthusiasm and passion as well. In case you are the subordinate: your success depends on how well you understand the goals of your boss and company and align your own role to those goals.

- You need to surround yourself with the right people. These are the people that positively and constructively support your goals. Negative people, complainers, people who say that it can't be done, and people that shy away from action, have no place in your team. Only engage people with the right mental attitude, as this can be the difference between success and failure.

- You need to have team players. People only looking out for themselves have their own goals in mind, different from your overarching goal. Let them chase their own dreams somewhere else.

- Maintain high standards for yourself and others. Ethics can't be compromised by anyone, as results obtained in a non-ethical way won't be lasting and eventually lead to failure. Always be polite to other people, there is no room for shouting, violence, swearing or abuse in a successful relationship. Treat others with respect, like you want to be treated. Be humane, warm and don't forget that you are dealing with other humans who have the same needs as you. The better you treat other people, the better things in life will come to you. It is the law of attraction.

- Invest in your people, just like you invest in your own self-improvement programme. When you invest in your people your reward will be increased loyalty and output. Provide them with the tools, knowledge, equipment, and education they need to advance. Because when they advance, they help you advance to your goal at the same time. Push for progress in your goals as well as in your people.

- Share the successes with the people that enable the successes. Acknowledge their contributions and reward them accordingly. Their success enables your success. Make your people successful and you will be successful.

Are you managing these key stakeholders and contributors in an appropriate way enabling progression to your goals?

Your success depends on the cooperation with other people
So align them with your grand vision
Engage people with the right mental attitude
Maintain high standards for yourself and other people
Invest in your people
Share the successes with your people

STEP 5

OVERCOMING OBSTACLES TO SUCCESS

Obstacles Create Learning And Business Opportunities

For most people the path to success resembles a long and winding uphill road with frequent detours and the occasional dead-end. It is how you handle these detours and dead-ends that define your success rate. All too easily people give up on their dreams and visions, just because an obstacle comes on their path, and they let themselves be side-tracked by the obstacle, instead of keeping their focus on the ultimate goal of their journey.

You need to be like bamboo: every day work hard to grow (your successes) and when a storm (obstacle) comes along, bend with the wind. Don't break when things don't go your way. Don't give up when you are facing a storm. Be persistent, because only those people who never quit become successful. If you quit, you will never be successful.

You are living a life that is highly dependent on other people. That means that in any of your activities you have connections with other people and organisations run by other people. Since you don't have 100 per cent control of everything that happens to you, you need to realise that life will bring you obstacles and problems and that you probably will go through general bad times, which will affect many other people as well. You need to realise that most of the time these problems and bad times have nothing to do with you or your abilities. So maintain your self-confidence, don't be shaken up and don't take it personally, even when the impact is personal.

Several types of external obstacles exist. Some obstacles are single events that impact only one person (a flat tire causing you to miss an important job interview), or a single event may impact many people (an earthquake damages the properties of many people). Then there are unfavourable circumstances, which are persisting over a longer period of time, affecting a single person (you are unemployed for a longer period of time), or affecting many people (a world-wide economic crisis). The difference between the bad event and the bad times is the duration. The bad event is a short time obstacle, whereas the bad times are prolonged situations of enduring obstacles. There is a reason to make these distinctions because of the opportunities arising from these obstacles:

- If a single event causes an obstacle only for you (event=flat tire, obstacle=how to get to or missed interview), then this creates a learning opportunity. The learning towards having more buffer time, regularly bringing the car to the garage, taking a different route, or taking public transportation.

- If a single event causes an obstacle for many people (event=earthquake, obstacle=property damage), then this creates business opportunities. The opportunities relate to cleaning, building, redecorating, gardening, transportation, security, temporary accommodations, financing, supplies or storage. Although you might have property damage as well, and be in the same situation as all the other people around you, if you are prepared to seize these opportunities, you may do really well, despite the bad times for everyone. In case you are severely impacted by the earthquake, you have learning opportunities as well, relating to the better preparation for the impact.

- In case of prolonged bad times for yourself (event=firing, bad times=longer time of unemployment), then this creates a learning opportunity. The learning towards expanding your skills to having better access to the job market, making use of a labour lawyer when being fired or better negotiation of termination pay. At the same time, the bad times may create new opportunities for you. You could consider to change career, become self-employed, take that long awaited vacation, develop new skills or take care of the children at home.

- In case of prolonged bad times for many people (event=bank crisis, bad times=longer time of recession), then this creates business opportunities. But you have to be prepared to seize such opportunities. When you are into real estate, and you are prepared, you can buy properties at enormous discounts compared to the height of the market. When you are an investor, you can buy stocks at largely discounted values. When you run outplacement services or a temporary labour agency, you have many good candidates to choose from. When you help people set up their own business, your services will be in high demand. You just need to be in the right line of business, and prepared to seize the opportunities. In case you are equally affected by the recession, you may have learning opportunities as well. What could have been done differently before the recession, to get through it without any negative impact?

The point is that each obstacle, negative event, crisis, emergency, or problem contains learning opportunities for those who are willing to analyse their own situation, and business opportunities for those who are prepared and ready to seize them.
What are you seeing in obstacles and bad times: the problem or the opportunity?

Therefore, never speak negatively about obstacles or problems. Firstly, everything is only temporary, and things become better again when you stay positive. Secondly, when you focus on negativity, you attract more negativity. Thirdly, when you focus on the problem, you're not focussing on the solution. Fourthly, each problem gives rise to opportunities.
How do you speak about your problems?

Be like bamboo
Every day work hard to grow (your successes)
When a storm (obstacle) comes, bend with the wind
But never give up and don't let it break you
Each obstacle or period of bad times contains
Learning opportunities and
Business opportunities
For those willing to see them

Your Thinking About Obstacles

You can have many problems thrown at you. But these problems are not your worst enemy. Your worst enemy is your own mind. Because when you keep these problems in your mind and let them cause negative thinking, you have already lost the challenge.

The way you think about obstacles determines how many obstacles you will encounter and whether you will be successful in overcoming these.

Think positively, and you overcome a reduced number of obstacles. Think positively, and you have smooth sailing towards success. Think negatively, and you have many obstacles on your path, which are difficult to overcome. Think negatively, and your pathway to success is full of hardship.
How are you thinking about obstacles?

Many people have been able to sustain a bad situation, find solutions to problems, find ways around, under or over obstacles, and emerge back on the pathway to success. Thinking success means understanding that obstacles are only there to make you stronger, to learn from, to build your character, and to prove to yourself and to the world that you have what it takes to be successful. Obstacles are not there to make you quit and give up. They are not there to make you despair and turn negative. If you think that obstacles come on your pathway for negative reasons, then you will see those obstacles as negative. Then you will let them negatively influence your success rate. Obstacles come on your pathway for a positive reason. You might be side-tracked from your goals without realising it. The obstacles serve the purpose to make you rethink where you are going, and whether you still are on the right path. Obstacles may put your passion to the test. Overcoming the obstacle strengthens your passion and resolution to succeed. In case you are finding many obstacles in your way: this may be a sign to change your way of thinking. Because thinking negatively about yourself and your chances to success brought these obstacles into your life in the first place. It is the law of attraction at work here, hampering any chance you might have of becoming successful.
Do you see the positive side of obstacles?

You need to control your thinking, by eliminating negative thoughts and only allow positive and constructive thoughts into your mind. Positive thinking is not dreaming or wishful thinking. Positive thinking supports the achievement of the goals by focusing on your goals and the concrete actions. It is not easy to remain positive in unfavourable times, but it is imperative that you do so. Thinking negatively during bad times only prolongs the bad situation and attracts more negative events your way. Thinking positively lets you focus on the solutions instead of on the problem, and makes you take actions to continue on your pathway to success instead of succumbing to unfavourable times. But that is not an easy thing to do. One main motivator will pull you through: it is your passion. Let your passion steer your thinking, as your passion keeps you motivated during times of difficulties and setbacks.
Is your passion for what you are doing strong enough to pull you through bad times?

Obstacles might come on your way, but never speak about them in a discouraging way. Keep the way you are thinking and speaking encouraging to yourself and your business. Don't admit the possibility of non-success to yourself or anyone else, and keep your verbal expression in line with your positive thinking. Your thinking should continue to focus on your progression towards your goals, even when you are in a situation in which you are not progressing or slipping back. This is just a temporary situation, and a positive attitude and persistence will pull you through this situation. Keep your belief, keep your desires, keep your passion, show gratitude for what you have already accomplished and keep taking focused actions to progress towards your goal.
How are you speaking about obstacles?

Though you must of course think positively about your success, you need to take into account that your success is linked to other people, and as other people don't always act like you need them to act, obstacles may come in your way. So don't expect to be successful 100 per cent of the time. Avoid being self-critical, avoid losing self-confidence, and avoid negative stress by realising that sometimes things don't go your way. You may experience set-backs, you may be skipped for promotion, you may fail the exam, you may get into a divorce, you may be made redundant from your work, you may miss the flight, you may fall ill, you may lose the business deal, you may lose a major client, you may get a horrible boss, etc. There are always circumstances beyond your control, and a successful person won't let his positive success thinking be negatively influenced by that.
Do you keep your thinking positive, despite obstacles?

Do not spend any time on thinking about what happens if you can't solve the problem, because then you are thinking in terms of problems instead of solutions. Do not spend too much time thinking about the obstacles, their impact or how difficult it is to solve them, but focus your energies on finding solutions. You need to spend time thinking about how you want the situation to be, not what your current situation actually is. Whatever the situation you are in, there are always things which are still good and positive. Concentrate on these and show appreciation for the things that are positive and enjoyable in your life. This will make you put the obstacle into the right perspective, and avoid that a crisis is blown out of proportion to the bigger scheme of what you are aiming for. Say to yourself that you have what it takes to find a solution and emerge even better out of the crisis. Convince yourself that the crisis is only temporary and strengthen your

resolve to be successful in achieving your goals. Put your subconscious mind at work to help you find solutions, as to how you can attain the desired state. Meditate on the desired state, and solutions will come to you. Talk to people who have gone through the same ordeal, and ask them for advice. Study and learn what you can about possible solutions and then put them to the test. When one approach does not work, move on to the next one, and so forth, until you succeed. To every problem there are multiple solutions. Find them, act on them, and you will be successful to continue on your path to the big prize of your life.
Are you positive about finding solutions? Are the problems or the solutions on the top of your mind?

The way you think about obstacles determines whether you are able to overcome them.
Think that it is not possible and you will fail
Think that it is possible and you will succeed
Think in terms of solutions instead of problems
Don't think about problems when they are unlikely
Think positive and keep faith

Overcoming Future Obstacles

One of the major success killers is the thinking about future obstacles. For example, you want to expand your skills and you are thinking of taking a difficult course concluded by a difficult exam for which many people fail. Do you see the exam as an obstacle, and do you chose an easier course or none at all? Your old boss retires and you get a new young boss. What if my new boss won't like me? What if my car gets a flat tire, and I won't make it on time for my interview? You are in a regular job, and are contemplating a change in career to become a writer. What if you won't sell enough books to make a living? Do such thoughts prevent you from making the career change? When you are pregnant: what if I am not a good parent? What if I won't get my child into that Kindergarten? What if my child won't get a scholarship? What if it rains on my wedding day? What if I fall ill during my vacation? What if my customers won't pay me? What if the bank won't give me that loan to start my business?

Future obstacles, risks, problems, stumbling blocks, obstructions, disadvantages, hurdles and hindrances can be divided into two categories: those that happen and those that don't happen.

Your mind can come up with as many possible future obstacles as it can conceive. If you let your mind run wild, it may come up with many reasons why these potential future obstacles are going to happen to you. Isn't it true that over the course of your life you have feared many future obstacles, risks and problems but only very few actually occurred?
Successful people handle possible future problems as follows:

- It is good to think about possible future obstacles, because that gives you the opportunity to plan ahead for a timely resolution of these problems. The better prepared you are when obstacles arise, the more efficient and effective your actions to overcome these obstacles. Other people will conclude that you are lucky in overcoming the obstacles, but in reality you were well prepared. Plan and take concrete actions today for the resolution of a future obstacle only when you see that without taking action now, that problem will definitely arise. If you see problems on your business horizon coming your way when you continue to do what you are doing now, then change your course today to avoid the problems or prepare yourself now to overcome the problems.

- Nobody knows for certain that they will be able to overcome all future problems. Also successful people don't have this certainty. But they do have one thing that helps them through the uncertainty of the future: confidence and belief in their success, belief that they will be able to overcome any obstacle, no matter how large and difficult. It is this belief that makes them look into the future and see success and great rewards, which are worthwhile all the efforts and hard work. They overcome their fears and doubts about future problems, as they know that such negative thinking only leads to failure. On the other hand, non-successful people (the people in Category I) look into the future and see failure and obstacles, which are not worth the efforts and hard work. So they stay where they are and are not able to advance in their life.

- Give no negative thought to possible future problems, obstacles, adverse circumstances, emergencies or disasters when there are no clear indications that these will actually occur. They may loom on your personal or business horizon, and may always stay on your horizon or even disappear altogether. Don't let your today's actions to success be influenced by such looming problems that are likely never to occur. You have time enough to prepare for handling or avoiding these problems when you see that these problems are in the process of materialising. You don't need to plan for a problem that is never happening in reality, when it only exists in your mind.

- No matter how significant and tremendous an obstacle may appear in the far future, do not give it that significance and importance in your present thinking. When you think positively and follow the success principles, you will see that the closer the obstacle, the smaller it becomes. A seemingly insurmountable obstacle in the far future may become a small and easy to overcome problem in the near future. The reason for this is the time factor. You are projecting yourself as you are now, as your situation is at present, into a problem that may be many years away. By the time when that future situation becomes your now and present, you won't be the same person anymore as you were when you saw that problem looming on your horizon. You advanced, you undertook action to succeed, you have prepared yourself for the situation, your circumstances have changed, which all make that once looming significant obstacle, insignificant in the present. The obstacle might actually still be of the same size as you saw it years ago, but your advancement and your preparations might have brought you in a situation where you don't see the obstacle as insurmountable anymore. You have outgrown the obstacle.

In summary, prepare yourself for future problems that may occur if you stay on your current pathway, but don't let possible future problems that might never occur influence your today's actions to become successful. This is how a Category III person thinks and acts, whereas a Category I person lets his fear for possible future problems, that might actually never occur, paralyse him to tread the pathway to success. At the same time, you do need to consider the risks. Risks are potential future negative events hampering your goal achievement. You need to be aware of the risks on your pathway,

and adequately manage those risks once their likelihood of occurrence becomes large enough to do something about them.
How do you think about possible future obstacles and problems? Do you let them paralyse your actions?

There are two sorts of future obstacles
Those that occur and those that don't
Don't let those that may never occur influence your today's actions in becoming successful
For those that could occur
Plan and take concrete actions to avoid them
Think positively that you will overcome them

Overcoming Existing Obstacles

The road to success never is a straight line. It is not possible to become successful without encountering problems, setbacks, resistance, criticism, disapproval, competition or even hostility. So expect problems, difficulties and obstacles. Don't be ignorant and expect your life to always go smooth and easy, but at the same time expect that you will be able to overcome any obstacle. Raise awareness of the fact that certain problems may arise on your path to success, and manifest your belief in your abilities to overcome those problems. It is your belief that will pull you through difficult times.
Is your belief strong enough to pull you through difficult times?

What do you do when you encounter an obstacle that seems insurmountable?

- Don't get upset or so emotional that you lose focus on the big prize. Calm your senses and rationally analyse the situation. What caused the problem to arise in the first place? What went wrong? What lesson can be learned from the situation? Learn what you can from the setback, look for the positive in the situation, and then look forward again. After having analysed and understood the problem, don't linger any longer than necessary, but concentrate on the solution. Let the solution be in your dominant thinking, not the problem.

- Every bad situation or problem happens for a reason. But that reason may not be obvious to you. You need to look at the situation or problem from the larger perspective of your life and goal achievement. Why did this situation come on your pathway to success? What positive take-away can you distil? A problem or bad situation is really just a neutral event coming into your life. It is your thinking that attaches a positive or negative value to it. So find the positive value in the situation or obstacle, and expect to see a positive side. The Universe is a friendly universe, and all things happen for a reason, even when you can't see or understand the reason. Often the reason is connected to your way of thinking, brought to your outward conditions by the law of attraction.

- Not under any circumstance let the difficulty of the problem convince you of failure, defeat or giving up. Tell yourself that there is a solution, that there is a way to get out of the bad situation. The law of attraction will attract solutions to your problem, consistent with your positive dominant thoughts. When you have the strong belief that there is a way out, then the right problem solving thoughts will enter your mind. Think that a solution is possible and solutions will come to you. On the other hand, when you tell yourself that you have failed and won't be able to overcome the obstacle, then that is exactly what will happen. An obstacle only becomes insurmountable, when you believe and think it is insurmountable. Refuse to accept that there is no solution to the situation, and never express to yourself that the situation is hopeless. There is always a way out. Consciously attract solutions by thinking that solutions are possible. Think that you are still on your way to success; the grand prize is still available at the end of your pathway. Keep your belief that you will achieve success and seize that grand prize. Express your belief by being persistent and never quit.

- Being persistent means that you keep trying to overcome the obstacle. If your solution for overcoming the problem does not work, even though you have tried many times, then still don't quit. Persistence is good, but when you are banging your head against a wall and don't get any progress, you need to change your approach to the problem. You need to come up with a different solution, and try out another way to get over, under or around the obstacle. In the mean time you must keep your eye on the goal, and keep in mind the reasons why you are undergoing the hardship. This keeps you motivated to keep trying in different ways.

- One way of helping you attain different solutions is to give it a rest. Often you may be so submerged into the details of the problem, that you lose the oversight and the big picture. Force yourself to zoom out again and rise above unimportant details. Put the solution aside for some time; sleep on it, and distract yourself with other things in the meantime. Get some physical exercise. Before going to sleep, submit the question of the resolution to your subconscious mind. Let your subconscious mind do the work for you, and before you know it, problem solving thoughts and ideas will enter your conscious mind. Then make a fresh start to tackle the problem, and you will be successful in finding a way to overcome the seemingly insurmountable obstacle.

- Find ways around obstacles one by one. Expect that you will be successful in achieving your goals, and that you will be able to tackle any problem or unfavourable situation that comes your way. Be resilient and bend with the wind, just like bamboo.

Understand that everybody goes through difficult times and has obstacles to overcome. The successful people of Category III go through such times without quitting. The successful people are not afraid of mistakes and obstacles, as they use them as learning opportunities. Negative experiences are the best teacher. Category III people keep their eye on the big prize, whatever the situation they are in.
How do you overcome seemingly insurmountable obstacles, bad situations and setbacks?

Sometimes an obstacle can be caused my mistakes. Mistakes made by you, or made by others. Nobody is perfect, so mistakes are bound to happen and it pays if you learn how to deal with them. Mistakes are unintentional but they still happen and can negatively influence your success. They may cause setbacks, crisis, emergencies or just annoyance. Don't let yourself be thrown off-balance by them. The causes for some mistakes may be simple and obvious, for some may be complex and diffused. Don't punish yourself for your own mistakes. Don't start a negative thinking pattern based on one mistake. Just ask yourself how this mistake could happen, and use it as a

learning opportunity to avoid similar mistakes in the future. Then let go of any negative thoughts about the mistake. Put a lid on the memory box where you store this mistake and move on. This is the way to advance your personality, career and business and move your life towards your goals.
What is your view on mistakes? Do you punish yourself or others for making them?

Some obstacles may seem impossible to overcome. You may have tried many times and different approaches, and still not move forward. Then perhaps the time has come to realise that you have your limitations. The way that you handle your own limitations determines whether you are going to be successful or not. If you keep pushing a topic over which you have limited knowledge, experience or capacity to come to a resolution, you risk frustration, despair or the negative thoughts of giving up. Don't do this to yourself. Instead, acknowledge that you have limitations standing in your way to success, and find ways to compensate for these limitations. Such compensation can be seeking advice from people who do have the required experience, or hiring other people that bring the qualifications to resolve the problem. Don't bash your head against a wall, when other people can easily assist you in overcoming the obstacle. You need to know yourself, in order to realise when you reach your limits.
Do you know your limitations? Do you accept them and find compensation so that you can continue on your pathway to success, or do you let them stop you?

Overcome existing obstacles in front of you
Predominantly think about the solution, not the problem
Understand the reason why something is happening
Find the positive in a bad situation or problem
Tell yourself there is a solution
Never think of giving up, bar those thoughts
Be persistent but try different solutions if needed
Tackle problems one by one, don't get overwhelmed
Zoom out of the details and take distance
See the bigger picture to get a good solution
Don't get bogged down by mistakes
Find compensation for your limitations

Overcoming Self-Created Obstacles

Many obstacles only exist in your mind. They do not exist in your outside environment, they are self-created and are only present within you. These obstacles relate to limiting beliefs, quitting too soon, impatience, seeing a setback as a failure, fear for losing what you have built up so far, self-depreciation, lack of confidence, insecurity, etc. You may have self-created excuses why something cannot be done: my health is not good enough, I am too old or too young, I don't have the right education, I am not intelligent enough, I am never lucky, I don't have the money, etc. These excuses are all rooted in fear, fear for failure.
What obstacles exist in your mind that are self-created blockages on your pathway to success? What excuses do you use to stall progress?

These are all self-created obstacles, rooted in fear. These obstacles can be successful in permanently blocking your way to success, if you let them. Your own thinking creates these obstacles. As your thinking is 100 per cent under your own control, you have the capacity and possibility to overcome these obstacles. But that only happens when you have the will to do so. A weak will is going to be eaten by the fears that linger in your mind, so that your fears can expand without any obstructions. A strong will is able to conquer those fears and push them out of your thoughts. When fear for failure is your dominant thought, you will fail. The law of attraction and your subconscious mind will attract and find reasons for you to fail. The excuses that fill your mind will be realised in practice. So the way out is to change your thinking. Clear your mind from the fears of failure and replace them with the thoughts of success. When you think success, irrespective of your circumstances of age, education, money, and health, then the law of attraction and your subconscious mind come up with reasons for you to be successful. They have you initiate actions that lead to success, while improving your education, wealth and health.
How do you handle your fears? Is your will strong enough to conquer them?

In most cases fears come from either bad experiences, bad advice from others or something unknown (uncertainty). You can eliminate the fears caused by bad experiences by rationally analysing the experience and finding reasons why there is no cause to fear a repetition of the experience. What were the special circumstances that led to the bad experience? Often such circumstances are unique and won't repeat themselves anymore. Don't let a

bad experience from the past become an obstacle on your path to success. Give yourself the reasons why it is not going to happen again. Perhaps you were not prepared well enough at the time? Then now do everything you can to prepare yourself. Perhaps you had not understood the circumstances at the time? Then now you can understand the circumstances by learning from this past event. Perhaps you were not concentrated on the topic at the time? Then now you can concentrate and turn the experience into a positive event. You took an exam, but failed and now you are afraid that you will fail again? Your failure can likely be linked to insufficient preparation, so this time, prepare yourself as well as possible and you will pass. You applied for a career step job and got rejected? So out of fear for more rejections you just stay in your mediocre job, without advancing in your career? Analyse why you got rejected, ask the interviewer for feedback, and understand the reasons. Then do everything you can to improve yourself, prepare yourself for the next interview at a career step company and you will succeed. It is really up to you to take a bad experience and turn it into something positive in your thinking. You won't make the same mistake twice, and make the new experience count on your path to success.
How are you learning from bad experiences? Can you turn them into new challenges to be overcome successfully?

Fears caused by bad advice from other people (other people telling you this is a bad idea and you won't be able to make it) are basically the same as fears for the unknown and its inherent uncertainty. These fears can be conquered by taking the following steps: learn as much as possible about the unknown situation or event, prepare yourself as best as possible, and then take action and tackle the thing you fear. Uncertainty about a situation will be reduced or eliminated altogether when you increase your knowledge about the event. So study hard for the exam, and your fear about not passing will be eliminated. Then go to the exam, go through the questions, and you will pass. You are afraid of public speaking and speaking up in meetings? Prepare for your presentation as well as you can. Understand what the audience wants to hear, why they are coming to listen to you. Analyse the behaviour of successful speakers, watch them on YouTube, and study them, or buy self-help guides on the topic. Then when you know what to do and what to say, have a public speaking event, and do speak up in the meeting. By actually doing the things you fear most you eliminate your fear. Fear exists only in your mind, and the action shows you that there is nothing to fear, so that your fear disappears from your thinking.
What actions do you undertake to conquer your fears?

Do you use any of the excuses of being too old or too young, not having the right skills or education, not having the money, not being healthy enough, or not being lucky? Your age, your level of education and your health themselves might not be self-created obstacles (they might have been inflicted on you by others or external circumstances), but using these as an excuse for not getting into action, is a self-created obstacle. The fact is that both old and young people become successful, so whatever your age, it is never too late or too early to start on your pathway to success. The point is that you need to make a start. Once you have started, every excuse you used to have disappears. Look at Mark Zuckerberg and other teenage millionaires. Just type "teenage millionaires" in your web browser, and you get a long list of names. Also late bloomers are successful. Nick Woodman became successful with his GoPro company when he was 38. Vera Wang started her own wedding dress brand line at the age of 40. Martha Stewart's success as home decorator started when she was 41. Colonel Sanders (Kentucky Fried Chicken) started his fast food restaurant franchise when he was 62. Jack Cover invented the Taser Gun when he was 50. It is never too late to start! Look at Jessica Cox (who has no arms) and Nick Vujicic (who has no arms and legs) who were able to become successful, despite, or rather because of, their physical disabilities. They turned a negative (physical) situation into a positive success. Most of the very successful people started without money. They just started with small steps, as much as they could afford within their budget and grew their money as they continued to grow their successes.
What are your self-created excuses?

These people never used their age, money or health as an excuse to not start doing what they love to do. And that is exactly the point: when you find your passion and put all your heart and thoughts into making that which you are passionate about successful, the thoughts of being too old or too young, your physical condition, your skill set or talents, are never going to be obstacles. When your heart is into what you are doing, you won't let anything hold you back. Your passion makes you start right away; your passion makes you overcome any obstacle. If you don't have the right skills or education, you acquire those skills and learn everything there is to know about the topic. If you were never lucky, it is because you were not prepared and did not create and seize the opportunities. So when you are passionate about what you are doing, you create your own luck by preparing yourself better than anyone else and creating the best opportunities to be successful. If you are not healthy, your passion makes you work hard to

improve your health, or learn to live with your physical disabilities and still be able to progress with your life.
What excuses do you still use that prevent you from embarking on the road to success?

To put this the other way around: if you continue to use the excuses of age, health, luck, education or intelligence, it simply means that you have not yet found your passion. So do everything possible to find your passion, and these excuses will disappear like snow for the sun. Find your passion, and you will be eager to start and realise your dream. It is never too early or too late to find your passion and follow its road to success.
What efforts are you putting into finding your passion?

Fears come into the minds of all people, whether you are a Category I, II or III person. It is how you handle your fears that makes the distinction. A Category I person lets the fears become his dominant thoughts causing a freeze of all actions to advance in life and towards success. That person succumbs to the fears and lets the fears determine his life, as a result of which he is not going anywhere. The mind of a Category III person is also regularly visited by thoughts of failure and fear for not being able to overcome obstacles. Also he regularly has self-created obstacles. But he won't let his fears control the direction of his life. He will notice these thoughts coming into his mind, rationally analyse them, and then discard these thoughts as not helpful for achieving success. He won't let them linger for a long time in his mind, to avoid that they take root. A person in this category will quickly refocus on thoughts of success. A Category II person was handling fears similar to a Category III person. But at a certain moment in his career, on his pathway to success, his thinking switched becoming similar to a Category I person. The fear of losing what he had built up has become stronger than the desire to continue advancing his life. His fears made him stall; they rooted in his mind.

It is easier to find excuses to quit; it is harder to find reasons to continue when you are facing obstacles and bad times. Show strength of character and rationalise away all those excuses. Find your passion and start taking actions. None of the self-created reasons is valid to postpone getting on the pathway to success. Most excuses are rooted in fear, fear for failure. If you let your fears guide you on your pathway to success, you won't get anywhere, as they will freeze all actions required to progress. When you use passion and purpose in life as your guiding star, you will continuously move forward on the pathway to success.

Are you letting your self-created fears guide you to success, or are your passion and purpose in life your navigator to success?

Many obstacles only exist in your mind
They do not exist in your outside environment
They are self-created and are only present within you
Excuses of age, health, luck, money, education or intelligence
They are rooted in fear for failure
Rationalise away all your fears and take action
Find your passion and you will overcome fears

Karma

All of us experience certain events in our progression towards goals, for which it is difficult to comprehend why they are happening to us. They don't seem to be in any relation to your goals and actions, they just seem to pop into your life, coming from nowhere, completely unexpected, completely independent from your thoughts and actions. Sometimes these events are strengthening your goal achievement, sometimes these events cause hurdles towards your goal achievement. They are the inexplicable events influencing your progression towards success. For example, you do your best to buy tickets to a local concert, but you aren't able to acquire any. At the night of the concert, a tornado crosses the stadium leaving many visitors wounded (but you weren't there). A large competitor acquires your company, they close down your department and after 25 years of being in the same team you are on your own. After a period of devastation, you set yourself new goals, and find new success as an independent consultant capitalising on your extensive experience. You fail to pass an exam, and need to take an extra course to master the subject where you meet the love of your life.
What were the events in your life for which it is difficult to understand why they occurred?

Your progression towards goals is not only influenced by the goals themselves, and your actions to achieve those goals, but also by an independent factor that can be called Karma. Karma is a term used in Buddhism, and describes the law of cause and effect from a spiritual perspective. When your thoughts and actions are positive, positive events will enter into your life, whereas when your thoughts and actions are negative, negative events will enter into your life. According to Buddhist beliefs, the Karma of your previous life can strongly influence your present life. In other words, positive and negative events might happen to you, for which you can't see a connection in your present life. You could also call this factor Fate or Destiny. Uncontrollable and unexpected events enter your life, requiring consideration in the analysis of the success principles.

Your progression towards success arising from the actions relate to the cause and effect generated by yourself, whereas the Karma element relates to the cause and effect of events which are generated outside your observable influence. It is up to you how you see your life: either as a continuous string of uncontrollable events leading nowhere, or as a highway to your life's success. Let me give some examples: When a person sets no goals for the progression in their life, and takes no actions to steer their life towards these goals, everything that happens to that person will seem like Karma. That person will feel like they live in an uncontrollable environment where (positive and negative) events just happen to them. This makes sense, because when you have no goals and no actions to progress your life, the Karma element automatically becomes the (only) driving force behind the events in that person's life. On the other hand, when you set clear goals and take all necessary actions to reach those goals, you will feel that you control and steer the progression and direction in your life, although certain unanticipated and uncontrollable events will still enter your life. But you won't feel overwhelmed by these events.
The stronger your goals and your actions to achieve these goals, the weaker the influence of Karma on your progression towards success.
How strong is the Karma element in your life?

Everything happens for a reason
Though you don't always understand the reason
Karma represents uncontrollable events
Outside your observable influence

The stronger your goals and your actions
The weaker the influence of Karma
On your progression towards success

Persistence

Many people never see success, because they give up too soon. They give up on achieving their goal when the going gets tough, when they experience setbacks, when they are going through bad times, when their family or friends tell them that they should give up or when obstacles come in their way that are seemingly insurmountable. Achieving rewarding goals needs time, effort and patience. Most of all it needs persistence, to never give up and pull through the bad times. Persistence means keeping your eye on the big prize in the future instead of on the problem directly in front of you. Persistence means to keep going with all the actions required to achieve your goal, irrespective of the hardship along the way. Persistence means holding on to your goal, and never give up on that goal. Still, goals may change from time to time. They change when you move from one phase in your life to the next phase, when there is a dramatic change in your own circumstances, or when you achieved your goal.
Are you persistent enough to get yourself through tough times?

You need to be persistent in the focus on your goals, as well as in the planning and execution of the actions that get you to your goal. But persistence does not mean charging ahead when it is time to change course. You need to stay flexible and be aware of changing circumstances, which may require you to change your actions for achieving your goal. Don't be like the Titanic and think that you are indestructible and keep on course when you are heading towards an iceberg.
Are you flexible enough to get yourself through tough times?

Your goals and actions are only as good as they were at the time when you made them. You need to be persistent in aiming for your goals and executing the actions, while at the same time being flexible enough to reassess, rethink and adjust your plan and goals when the circumstances

dictate. The whole society continues to develop, your external conditions continue to develop, and when you are too rigidly holding on to out-dated goals and actions, you may never become successful and even fail big. Sony sold the Walkman portable music players from 1979 till 2010. If they would have held on too long to their goal of the Walkman, they would have run out of business when the Apple IPod came on the market at the end of 2001. Kodak slept through the digital revolution and resisted change to new technologies. They maintained their old goals and plans, and as a result went bankrupt in 2012, after 130 years pioneering in film industry.
Are you persistent and at the same time flexible? Do you regularly re-evaluate your goals and plans and make adjustments when necessary?

The opinions expressed by other people often are the biggest challenge to your persistence. We all value the views of our spouse, family, friends, bosses and other people that play an important role in our life. Because of the importance of our relationship with them, they have a significant influence on our persistence to chase a goal. How often have these people told you that the risk is too high, that it can't be done, that you are a fool believing you can escape your mediocre life, that you should not put at risk your comfortable life, that you will need a miracle to pull this off, that you don't have the knowledge, that you don't have the money, etc.? Many people then stop in their tracks and give up on whatever inspiring and passionate goal they had, and get sucked back in a meaningless and boring routine life. But you should not let other people destroy your dreams; don't give them this power over you to do so. Most of these people don't know or understand your passion, and make such remarks out of ignorance. Good advice is advice that helps you achieve your goals. Advice that you should quit because they don't understand your passion or your goals, or because your goal deviates from their goal (for you), is advice to be ignored. Don't let other people rattle your persistence on your way to success.
How do you handle advice from people close to you? Do you let them influence your persistence in living a purposeful and successful life?

Another condition that weakens your persistence is when times are good, and everything goes smooth and easy. When you experience success after success and all good things come your way without much effort, your persistence will likely wane. You start taking it easy, you lose focus, you become easily distracted and your persistence will decrease. You start doing other things non-related to your goals, you start hanging out with the wrong crowd and your thoughts are on many topics not related to your main goals. Successes weaken persistence. Unless you are at the end of your life, and

your candle is soon blown out, that is fine. But when you still have many productive years ahead of you, that is a disaster. You must stay persistent and focused on your goals, even when times are good. Your good times are the result of hard work and persistence from the past; they form the basis of your present success. The harvest you reap today was sown in the past. Your investment of today will pay off in the future. If you want to be successful also in the future, you need to keep your focus and persistence on your goals. When times are good and you are successful, set bigger goals, and be persistent on those larger goals. If you want to extend the good times as long as possible, you must keep working on them. Stop working on your goals and your good times will quickly turn into bad times. So be persistent also when everything is coming your way.
Are you persistent enough when times are good to sow the seeds for future successes?

Your persistence is also put to the test by rejection, by the fact that you never have the certainty that you will indeed be successful, by difficult problems, setbacks and obstacles. The way to overcome these challenges is dealt with in the other steps in this book. You need persistence to keep your passion, your enthusiasm and your love for what you do. Much of this persistence is based on your willpower. The strength of your willpower in combination with your desire for something better and a purposeful life will keep you going. In this respect you can say that persistence consists of willpower combined with determination and flexibility.
What does your persistence consist of?

Many people never see success because they give up
Persistence means having the willpower to pull through
It means being determined never to quit
It means being flexible to adjust to changing circumstances
When times are difficult and obstacles block your way

STEP 6

MEASURING AND REVIEWING PROGRESS

Monitoring Progression

One of the main sources for happiness is the striving for and progression towards meaningful and challenging goals. The more meaningful and the more challenging the goals, the higher the feelings of happiness when you are indeed progressing towards those goals. Measurement of progress towards your goals is also important for another reason. Regularly measure your progress against your predefined planning. Are you lagging in progress? Think about ways to get back on track, by taking more actions, or taking different actions when the previous actions do not seem to be effective enough. Review the effectiveness and efficiency of your actions with a high frequency, e.g. daily, weekly, monthly or at any other pre-determined interval. When your progress is lagging, analyse its reasons and improve on the factors that are causing the delay. Look at new ways to do something better, and think creatively.
Are you taking joy and pleasure out of your progression towards your goals? Do you systematically measure and review your progress at pre-set intervals? Do you take timely corrective actions when your progress is lagging?

Systematically measure and review your progress
Take timely corrective actions when progress is lagging
Look at new ways to do something better, think creatively
You can't be too rigid and block yourself from new ideas

Keeping Momentum And Focus

Obstacles, problems, and crisis are likely going to stall your progress towards your goals. It is all too easy to let these obstacles influence your focus and momentum. They can cause smaller or larger distractions that make you think about the problem at hand instead of getting back on track to your goals. You want to be successful? Then you need to keep focused and keep your momentum, even when things don't work out the way you want them to.

You can keep your momentum by keep on doing all the other things that keep you on track to your goals. The achievement of your goals never depends on the success of one single event. Therefore, it will never depend on one single setback either. Diligently work off each single obstacle at a time, while you keep moving forward on all the other activities that bring you closer to your goals. Don't put a stop to all your activities, because one of them causes a problem or setback. Keep your momentum by building on those actions that move you closer to your goal.
Are you able to keep momentum? Do you do the right things to keep moving forward?

What you are doing today builds the foundation for your future success; the more you do today, the stronger your foundation is going to be. At times obstacles may shake your foundation, but as long as you keep adding substance to your basis, it will become strong and carry your success.
Keep your momentum going, and don't let obstacles deter you from moving forward towards your goals. When you love what you are doing, and you are doing what you love, your passion for your goals will push you forward. Your passion keeps your momentum moving, as you won't let a single obstacle question your belief that you are doing the right things for the right reasons. If you let an obstacle stop you, you will lose momentum and you run the risk of losing everything that you have built. The latter will happen when you let the obstacle convince you that you should give up. Because when you quit, you voluntarily let go of everything that you have invested up to that point. All the hours, days, months and years spent on achieving your goal will have been for nothing. Your return on investment will be zero or even negative. You will have wasted energy on things that did not help you advance in your life, career, business or relationship.
Is your passion driving your momentum? Do you keep investing in your future success?

There may be situations where your momentum does come to a standstill. The times and circumstances may be averse to what you are trying to achieve, the whole industry might be in a crisis, your product might not find any buyers in the market, the economy might be in recession, you might not have the money to proceed, or other resources might not be available. Like every person, you might be thinking of quitting because you don't see any improvements to your situation in the foreseeable future. Still, you need to keep doing everything else to keep yourself on your pathway. Even though your today's actions might not show pay-off for a while, keep doing what

brings you joy and passion and makes you feel good. Prepare yourself for when the times become better again so that you are ready to seize the opportunities when they arise. Be better prepared than all your competitors and you will be the one that is successful as soon as the tide turns. You will see that momentum will slowly restart, even if the obstacles remain in place. Find other ways to pick up the pace again and let your passion drive your momentum, and things will improve again. Everything in life is impermanent; it is just a matter of time perspective. If you have a micro-perspective, bad times may seem like forever. If you have a macro-perspective on your life, bad times are short and inevitably make place for good times.
Do you continue to build a strong foundation for success, even when progress has stalled?

One of the reasons for your momentum to come to a standstill can be your loss of focus. Loss of focus may be caused by distractions such as crisis and setbacks, or by distractions that have nothing to do with your core problems or obstacles. It is only human to focus on the problem at hand instead of keeping your focus on a goal that is still many years away in the future. It makes sense to concentrate on that what is immediately in front of you as a matter of survival. While you are concentrating on finding solutions for the immediate obstacle, you still need to keep your eye on the ultimate goal. In order to be successful you need to reach your goal, and that means overcoming the obstacle in front of you. The resolution to the problem must move you forward and put you back on track towards your goal. Keep your focus on the big prize and don't let bad times or obstacles let you forget why you are doing what you are doing.
Are you able to maintain focus on the big prize, despite the adverse circumstances?

When you meet an obstacle, don't stall
Keep your momentum by building on other actions
That move you closer to your goal
Momentum may be lost by distractions or loss of focus
Refocus and keep your eye on the big prize
Keep doing all you can to progress towards your goal

STEP 7

ACHIEVING SUCCESS

The Feelings Of Success

From a biological point of view, success is a personal feeling of positive emotions created by the release of certain chemicals in the brain. Dopamine is released in the brain when you are seeking the feelings for rewards from setting and achieving goals, triggering curiosity, expectation, anticipation, excitement, learning and desire, promoting advancement of your personal life. This is one of the reasons why people want to be successful. It creates these pleasurable feelings of happiness, achievement, excitement, relief and satisfaction.

On the other hand, failure induces negative feelings of disappointment, self-depreciation, despair, sadness, frustration, regret or anger. Nobody wants to feel the emotions caused by failure. It is up to you to avoid them, and you can avoid them by controlling your thinking. Never allow yourself to think that you have failed, or listen to other people claiming that you have failed. Keep believing in yourself and keep following your passion to a worthy and meaningful goal.

The feelings of success and failure are an effect. In case you want to have more of the success feelings and avoid the failure feelings, you need to change the cause. The cause is your thinking. Any event in your life is neutral. It is your thinking that labels an event as positive or negative, as success or failure. So control your mind with respect to the labelling of events, think only positively and success, and you are going to be able to avoid the feelings of failure. As nobody is perfect and even the most successful people are prone to negative thinking at times, you need to observe when negativity enters your mind. When it does, understand why this is the case, learn from it, and then discard the negativity and turn back to your dominant positive thoughts. This is going to avoid that the negative feelings of failure take root.
Are you enjoying the feelings of success? Do you want to have more of these feelings? What do you do to discard your negative thinking?

Chemicals in the brain cause the feelings of success
They generate positive, pleasurable, exciting feelings

Success feelings are good and you can have more of these
Feelings of success or failure are the effect
The cause is your thinking
Think only positively and generate success feelings

Celebration Of Success

Success comes in many forms, sizes and with different frequencies. Success may be the achievement of a big project that lasted for multiple years, such as the completion of your Bachelor degree at University. Success may be losing 20 pounds of weight within 10 weeks' time. Success may be the completion of the 6-hour hiking trail. Success may be the completion of 10 hours of community service. Success may be finishing reading this book. There are many ways in which success can be defined, and each person will have their own way of measurement. There is one thing, though, which all these measurements have in common: there is an underlying timeline from the moment a goal is set, till the moment of completion. This timeline may be hours, days, weeks, months, years or even decades. Particularly with the very long timelines of years and decades, it is important to identify intermediate points of success, the achievement of milestones along the path to completion, and not wait with the acknowledgement of success only when the end-goal has been achieved.
What are the intermediate points of success for your goals?

We humans have an inherent need for regular confirmation of what we are doing is right and each human longs for confirmation on a regular basis that they are living a meaningful existence on Earth. One way of confirming this meaningful existence is the determination that you are making progress towards worthy goals. It is the frequency of this confirmation, which comes into play when the timelines of your goals are very long. The lower the frequency of confirmation, the more difficult it will be for you to maintain belief in that what you are doing is the right thing. This may lead to frustrations, reduction of motivation, weakening of actions to achieve the goals, etc. So it is important to maintain a reasonably high frequency of confirmation of the progression. Determining milestones along the path to

goal completion and subsequently measuring your progress at these milestones can create this confirmation of progress. Such measurement points provide opportunities for assessing whether the quality and quantity of the actions are sufficient to attain the final goal, or whether corrective actions need to be initiated. It is at these pre-set milestones where celebrations of intermediate successes are appropriate.
Are you celebrating success whenever you can?

Celebrate your intermediate successes. Share your celebrations with those people who have provided valuable contributions to your intermediate goal achievement. Celebrate the small things. Celebrations come in all sorts of ways and sizes. Celebrations do not have to be big. Small tokens of appreciation and acknowledgements often already accomplish much. The point is to celebrate regularly, and not let intermediate achievements pass by without recognition. Regular celebrations of successes will keep your goal energy high and it will keep yourself and those contributing to your goal focused. It can serve as a re-iteration of what you are doing is the right thing, is well on its way, and is worthwhile doing.
Does celebration of success give you a positive boost?

Remember that feelings of success are extremely pleasurable feelings. Get into the habit of increasing the frequency of release of these brain chemicals, and increase the frequency of feeling pleasure, excitement, relief and satisfaction. Increasing the frequency of celebration of intermediate successes will thereby lift your happiness level.

Recognise successes
Determine intermediate milestones
To increase your frequency of celebrations
As this will strengthen your goal energy and focus
And give you pleasurable feelings of happiness

Sharing Of Success

Due to the interconnectivity and interdependence of the modern world, success is seldom possible without interaction with other people. It depends on the active support from other people in executing actions and progressing towards your goals. Your goals are completely yours, created in your own mind, driven by your own desires and beliefs, but actions to progress towards those goals are unlikely independent of other people. Take the example of your goal to get rich. Getting rich means increasing your possession of money, by increasing the flow of money towards you. And where does money come from? Assuming that you don't have a licensed money printing press at home, money will need to come from other people. Other people must be willing to give you money. As most people don't give you money for nothing, you must give these people something in return. So the achievement of your success in getting rich is dependent on the value of your services/products that you provide to other people. Take other examples; such as your goal to have a successful career, your goal to be in a loving relationship, your goal to achieve a sports award. You need subordinates, peers, bosses, your partner, your coach to help you succeed. *Are you clear about who else are responsible for your success?*

Success never comes from your own efforts only. So make it a habit to share your successes, as other people will have provided a contribution to your success. When you want to be successful time and time again, then share the results of your success with those who provided an important contribution to your goal achievement. This is the law of attraction at work. If you share your success with other people, you will attract more success to yourself. The more people benefit from your success the more success will enter your life. That is because the sharing of success multiplies the volume of the thoughts and beliefs generating your success. The other people will carry your success in their mind, and this creative force will increase the support for actions to achieve your goal. These other people will think of ways for you to attain your goal. They will initiate actions, which directly or indirectly help you succeed. Keep success to yourself, and nobody else will attach value to it. Share success with others and other people will give it a value for themselves, which causes them to put in efforts, initiate actions to capture that value for themselves. Success improves your life, and sharing success improves the life of other people as well. Sharing success is a form of gratitude to those people who enabled your success in the first place.

Do you have the habit of sharing your success and acknowledging the other people who contributed to your success?

Sharing of success can take many forms. It could be acknowledging (personally, formally or publicly) those people who were critical in achieving your goal. For example, when a team achieved the successful completion of a project, the manager should acknowledge all the members of the team for their contribution to the goal achievement. This can be done individually, but much more powerful is the acknowledgement in front of the whole team and the (internal or external) customers for which this project was executed. This has a dual impact: it rewards and puts in the spotlight those people who worked towards a common goal and helped achieve this common goal, plus it will generate goodwill in the form of belief and trust for their support in achieving the next goal.
In what way do you share your success?

It could be sharing the spoils of victory with those who supported you through difficult times. When your goal was to generate a significant amount of money (by completing a project, winning a case, selling a house, selling of stocks, receiving a bonus) and you are successful, share some of the money with those people who supported you. Even sharing your money with people who need it more than you do, will bring more money to you. Share some of the money with charity or other good causes. Although there might be no link between your goal achievement and these people in need, sharing your success will bring more success to you. It is the law of attraction at work. And this will work independently of whether you believe in it or not, as it is one of the neutral laws in the Universe.
Are you sharing your success with people that are in need? Do you give to charity as a means of giving back to society?

Success never comes from your efforts only
Other people contribute to your success
Acknowledge them and share your successes with them
Share your success through charity as well
And more success will come to you
It is the law of attraction at work

Luck Has Nothing To Do With Success

I am sure that you have heard other people say that someone had a lot of luck and that this luck caused him to be successful. Or rather, many people relate this to themselves in a negative way. They say that they are not successful because of bad luck. They use the word good luck to explain seemingly uncontrollable positive external events, whereas bad luck is used for seemingly uncontrollable negative events. This is, however, a misconception rooted in their thinking process and their understanding of the underlying principles of success. The people that use the words of bad luck are usually looking for excuses justifying their non-success, without having the courage or comprehension to admit that the root cause of failure lies with them. Therefore, (good or bad) luck is a concept rooted in ignorance. It is the ignorance for the fact that luck does not relate to something coming out of nothing. It does not relate to something over which you have no influence. It does not relate to something which only happens to other people (when luck is considered positive, good) or which only happens to oneself (when luck is considered negative, bad).
Do you use the words of good luck or bad luck?

How to overcome this way of thinking? The following equation says it all:

Good Luck = Preparation + Opportunity
Bad Luck = no Preparation + no Opportunity

These equations can be explained as follows. Good luck happens to you when you are well prepared and you seize the opportunity to execute what you prepared for. Preparation is fully under your control. The better you prepare yourself (for exams, meetings, relationships, sports, etc.) the better you will perform during the events. Opportunities are the events for which you prepared yourself. Opportunities can be strongly influenced as well; they can be created, developed, groomed. You have the power to create the events and circumstances where you can shine with your high level of preparation. So in effect, preparations as well as opportunities are under your own control, and thus there is no such thing as good luck that is fully outside your scope of control.

The similar concept applies for bad luck. If you don't prepare yourself for meetings, exams, relationships or sports, you are likely going to fail when such event requires you to show your best performance. Your best performance will likely be below your own and other people's expectations, and you will fail to achieve your goal. Equally, when you do prepare yourself, but you don't create or seize opportunities to show how good you are, you will fail to achieve your goal as well.

Some people say that others create their own luck. But what they are really saying is that these people create their own success, through preparations and opportunities. In essence, you can substitute the words Good Luck by Success, and Bad Luck by Failure. This shows that luck is not a determinant factor in your success, but preparation and opportunity are:

Success = Preparation + Opportunity
Failure = no Preparation + no Opportunity

So if you want to be successful, do your preparations and create and seize opportunities, and forget about the word luck. The words good luck and bad luck have no place in your dictionary when you are seeking to be successful.

The harder you work at preparing yourself and the harder you work at creating and engaging with opportunities, the more successful you will be. Obtain more experience, through practice, and spend more hours studying than anyone else, and you will be more successful than other people. When you put in more hours studying for your exam and take more practice tests than anyone else, spend more hours on the driving range than anyone else, read more books about raising children than anyone else, spend more hours in the fitness than anyone else, obtain more degrees and certificates for your profession than anyone else, you will be much more successful than anyone else and you will be able to achieve big goals.
Are you doing everything you can to be successful? Are you well prepared and do you create and seize opportunities?

Some people might say: you will be luckier than other people; you are creating your own luck. When these people see successful people, they only see the end result, i.e. the success. They don't recognise the hard work that a successful person had to put in, in order to achieve the end result. Oftentimes the success is then attributed to luck, while the hard work for the preparations remains unacknowledged. This topic is often times exaggerated in the media. TV programmes, advertisements and movies often depict super successful people, such as musicians, Internet

billionaires, movie stars and teenage millionaires, and show their great successes (and significant wealth accumulation) these people have achieved. The media glorifies their successes and creates an expectation that there is a quick and easy way to become successful and wealthy. But the reality is that there is no instant and effortless way to super success, wealth, power and admiration. Such instant successes happen seldom, and only to a few extraordinary talented people who seize the right opportunities. For everyone else, super success and wealth accumulation can be achieved, but only through hard work. Don't be fooled by what the media is presenting you about success. You need to follow your own path, you need to put in harder work than others, you need to prepare yourself better than other people, and then you will be more successful than other people, and with the right opportunities, you might become super successful (and wealthy) yourself. This is the only way. Other people will then tell you how lucky you were in achieving what you have.
Are you creating your own luck?

Luck is not a determinant factor in your success
As luck does not exist
Putting in hard work for preparations
And seizing the right opportunities bring success

Creating The Appearance Of Success

Display your success, even before you are successful. Behave like a successful person, while you are busy paving the way to your success. Other people will see you as a successful person, because first and foremost they judge you on your appearance. Show behaviour of success, dress for success, groom your outward appearance to success, and people will treat you like a successful person. This has a double effect. People connect your outward appearance to one of being successful, knowing that the outward appearance reflects how you feel inside. This outward appearance will strengthen your inner success feelings and your thinking that you have already made it. Anyone can do this, even with a small budget. It is quality that counts in the outside appearance, not quantity, so spend five to ten times your usual amount on pieces of clothing and accessories, but buy only a fraction of the usual quantity. Go first class with a select few material items that you carry around, and people will give you a first class treatment of someone already being successful. If you always bought $300 suits, instead of buying several of those, buy only one which is $3'000. In case the shoes in your rack cost on average $100, buy one pair for $800, to match your expensive suit. In case you've always bought handbags for around $150, buy that one bag for $1'500 and carry it around with style. Your haircut costs you $30 at the local hairdresser once every two weeks? Have yourself groomed in style by the best hairdresser in town once in a while. In case your watches used to cost around $250, buy that one world-class watch for $4'000. In case you are traveling with a $150 suitcase that needs to be replaced every two years, buy that $1'000 high-end aluminium suitcase. Not only will that suitcase last longer than 10 years, you will also look cool as a world traveller. You never carry more than $100 cash in your wallet? Start carrying $1'000; it doesn't mean that you need to spend all that cash, just keep your spending level the same. It will make you feel like you already have all the money you need, and other people will think that you are successful in your business. Remember, it is all about appearance. When you have a cupboard full of $40 polyester shirts to wear with your suits, get one with cuffs made-to-measure for $400, and buy a nice set of cufflinks. These first class products have first class quality, and are going to last much longer than your cheaper products. Some first class products like branded watches or handbags can even be for life and can be passed on to your eager teenagers when you yourself go bigger. You might not have the budget to spend on all first class products simultaneously, but you can plan for a gradual change in appearance. Don't get yourself into debt though. Even when this takes several years, plan for it and make it one of your goals. People around you, at work, in the family, at the club, your friends, will soon enough notice changes and positively comment on your improving style. They will tell you that you must be doing very well, and that you must be very successful. And this is exactly what you want to achieve, because people will look at you differently, new opportunities for success will open up. Create the appearance of success, and everyone you meet will treat you as a successful person. Your outward appearance of success makes you feel good about yourself. It gives you additional self-confidence, creates the feelings of success and strengthens your persistence to achieve success.

How is your appearance? Does your appearance reflect style, first class and success, or do other people see you as a mediocre person who can barely make it through life?

You do not yet have the outward appearance of a successful person? Set up your self-improvement programme. Decide how it is that you want to look like when you have achieved your goals. Compare this to how you look like now in terms of clothing, accessories, haircut, car, travel and other ways of appearance. Then look at the gap, and based on your available budget, start closing the gap. Don't listen to criticism of others regarding your change in style. You are doing this for yourself, for achieving your own goals. These changes will make you feel good about yourself, and your own feelings are the ones that count in this respect. Criticism about your changed appearance by your immediate environment is caused by insufficient understanding of what you are trying to achieve. Try to lift their ignorance or disregard their critique.
Have you ever thought about improving your outward appearance? Can you pinpoint yourself what needs improving, or do you need advice from a trusted person to set the direction? Are you able to plan and execute your self-improvement programme?

Similarly, you need to think of yourself as a successful person, because you are what you think you are. Even when you are in a job, which is of limited interest to you, or a job that is still at a low level, you need to think that your job is important, and that you are important for this job. You need to think and show appearance that you are making your job a success, and never talk negatively about it. Your bosses will never promote you when you talk negatively about your daily work, your position, your colleagues, your role or the company you work for. A new company won't hire you when you talk negatively about your old job, boss or company. Think of yourself as being stuck in a mediocre position with nowhere to go, and you will carry this to your outward appearance, which your bosses, peers and subordinates will pick up very quickly. People who always complain will stay where they are, and be the first ones selected for the downsizing programme. So even when you are in a job where you don't want to be, create the appearance of positivity, enthusiasm and success, and soon you will be asked to move to something better, as your bosses are going to think that you are too good for that job and can add more value to the company in a position with a larger scope. A new company will gladly hire you for a bigger position when you talk positively and enthusiastically about your old company, bosses and the successes you achieved there. But be careful in creating this job appearance. It must be rooted in the truth and reality. If you overdo it you will be seen as arrogant, exaggerating or a hot air balloon. Other people will quickly notice whether your appearance is genuine or not. If it is not genuine but played, your hot air balloon will be popped, and you will achieve the opposite of what you set out to achieve: you will fail. So really think and convince yourself that your job is important and that you are important for the job, even when it is not your ideal job. You have chosen the job for a certain reason. Hopefully the reason was that this job is one of many steps towards your life's goals. Think of it as a challenging hurdle to be conquered, as just temporary hardship on your pathway to success, and make the best of it. Keep your eye on the big prize further down the pathway to success, and keep doing everything you can to advance yourself, which must include being successful in your present (non-ideal) job. Nothing is permanent in life, and you can move to a more ideal job when opportunity comes. It is up to you how long it takes till this opportunity arrives.

How is your job appearance? Are you thinking of yourself as successful, and do you appear successful? Is this authentic and genuine, even when you don't really like the job? Do you speak positively about your company, bosses and colleagues?

Create the appearance of success
Let other people think you are already successful
Dress for style, quality and show first class
Think of yourself as already successful
Show and talk success in your job appearance
Show other people your positivity
And your appearance will become reality

The Time Between Start And Success

For most people success does not come overnight. This means that the period between your initial start on the road to success and the attainment of the success has a certain duration. The length of this duration is strongly influenced by the factors covered in this book. These are factors such as your belief, the concreteness of your goals, the persistence and focus of your actions, etc. The stronger these factors, the shorter the period between start and ultimate success. The bigger your goal is, the longer the period between start and ultimate success will be. This period may range anywhere between several months, years or your lifetime.

Is it worthwhile to strive for a goal that may take 5, 10, 20 or even 30 years to achieve? Yes, it is! Because the goal at such a level is usually the single biggest goal in your life, reflecting the ultimate purpose in your life on Earth. Such a goal will capture your all-consuming passion, which gives you so much energy and drive, that time seems to fly by.

If you need to be convinced that the duration of 10 or 15 years to the goal is worthwhile pursuing, then you have a goal that is not suitable for you (somebody else, like parents, spouse, family might have "convinced" you of this goal, or you have not yet sufficiently thought it through). Because when you are super passionate about a certain goal, you will automatically have all the belief, and you will be willing to spend all the time needed to achieve that goal. Look at the example of James Dyson.
What is the duration in achieving your goal? Do you have a really long-term goal, representing the purpose in your life, or does the long-term duration to achieve your goal put you off?

It is not possible to layout the exact day-to-day path to a goal that is 10 or 15 years in the future. The reason is that society changes, you change and the pathway will change. You can, however, make a high level roadmap to your goal, break this roadmap down into sections, and set intermediate goals to be attained at the end of each section. You can then create a hierarchy or pyramid of goals, so that success at the intermediate goals will eventually lead to the achievement of the highest, top, goal. This breaks down the long period for achieving your goal into multiple sections of shorter periods, which are easier to oversee, control, plan and execute. Apply the good principles of project management by using milestones, actions, progress measurement, and corrective actions for deviations. The shorter periods have another positive impact: they enable you to reach intermediate successes along the way to the big prize. The more you can realise success along the way, the stronger your motivation to push on to the next milestones. Feelings of success will breed feelings of wanting more of those feelings. So don't look at your lifetime goal as one of an insurmountable mountain in the faraway distance, look at it as a series of smaller conquerable hills of which the first one is very close to you. Stack all the small hills together and you will have your mountain!
Did you break down your long-term goal into smaller manageable steps? How long is the duration for achieving a goal of the intermediate sections?

Even when you reach your ultimate success, when you live the purpose of your life, when you live your passion, you will still be ever so engaged with your goal. Achieving success does not, and should not, mean that suddenly everything comes to a standstill, that you sit on your laurels and retire from the activity for which you worked so hard and long. If that is the case, it is not your real passion and the purpose of your life (anymore). For when you achieve your passion and the purpose of your life, you will want to keep doing that activity, especially when you have become successful. When you have become successful, you will look for bigger goals and enduring success to make an even bigger positive impact on society. Thus, the achievement of one big goal will lead to the setting of an even bigger goal. At that very high level, the goals are gradually shifting, and will direct their focus on the greater good through philanthropy. Well-known examples are Bill Gates, Warren Buffet and George Soros, who each donated many billions to charity and disease research institutions.

The message is that when you are a person who strives for success through goals, that goal setting and successes are likely to continue for the rest of your life. Naturally it will end when your life ends. And even then, your legacy may continue through foundations and descendants carrying on the good work.

What kind of person are you? Are you satisfied with achieving small successes and then stop, or are you always hungry for bigger successes and do you set yourself ever-bigger goals?

Success does not come overnight
It may take 10, 15, 20 years or a lifetime
It is worthwhile to strive for a goal that may take that long
When this goal reflects your ultimate purpose in life
And captures your all-consuming passion
Giving you energy and drive, so that it seems that time flies

WHEN
TO
QUIT

Throughout this book I have been making the point in persisting in your goal achievement and to never giving up. However, there are special circumstances in which you should consider quitting what you are trying to achieve. There may be some causes that should make you question whether it is still worthwhile to pursue your goal. These causes are neither the doubts, uncertainties or difficult situations or obstacles, nor are they other people's advice to do something else. As long as you love what you are doing and are doing what you love, you should keep chasing your big goal, despite what life is throwing at you.

This all changes when you have lost your passion, when you don't like what you are doing anymore, when you are in a transition phase from one phase in your life to another, causing a shift in how you see the purpose in your life. When you have no passion anymore for what you are doing, you should give up and cease chasing the big goal, because you will likely never achieve it. The lack of passion, the change in your thinking, makes the goal unattainable. Your personal or business circumstances might have changed, which may cause your life's big goal to change. Such change in circumstances may bring about a change in your thinking, a change in your career goals, a change in your life's priorities. When such changes result in a reorientation of your future, your passions may shift as well. This shift in passion is not something negative. You should see it as positive. You may be reinventing yourself, you may be transforming your life, you may be evolving into a different person, you may be reordering your life's priorities, or something similar. Instead of foolishly continuing to strive for out-dated goals, give up on your old goal and set a new goal consistent with your reordered priorities. Set the new goal in harmony with your new passion, and you will be back on track to success.

There is a second reason that may force you to give up on your goal. That is when you have exhausted all possibilities, after trying hard and after experimenting with your approaches, to find a solution. When it is clearly evident that there is no way around, under or above the obstacle, you should think hard about the reason why this is happening to you. Putting energy into a cause, without achieving the cause, is wasting energy. In nature nothing ever is wasted. So you need to think again whether your energy is better put to use for a different purpose than overcoming the obstacle. Everything in your life happens for a reason. So when the obstacle indeed is insurmountable, put this obstacle in the bigger perspective of your life. What do you see? Is the Universe trying to tell you that you are entering a dead-end? Is it telling you that your life will turn out even better when you make a change in course? Is it telling you that you have been blind for certain things, which are going to lead to failure in the future? When you are not getting what you want, when you are not achieving your goal despite all your efforts, it might be that something bigger and even grander awaits you, and that you need to be patient till that something bigger arrives. The timing might not be right, you might be in the wrong place, or in a relationship with the wrong people. Perhaps you should consider to temporarily postpone all actions for this specific goal, until the circumstances are favourable again. Put it on hold until you see a chance to be successful.

The other alternative is that perhaps you simply need to accept that the obstacle is insurmountable and move on. Your pride might be hurt, your feelings might be wounded, you might be in emotional pain, you might be suffering or in distress, but all these negative emotions should not be the force behind the decision to call it quits. You should only call it quits when rationally there is no other solution than to accept the situation or obstacle in your way. Leave your negative emotions out of this decision process. When there is no other way than to accept the situation, then do that and move on. It helps if you can learn to forget, avoiding that negative emotions and situations keep lingering in your mind. There is no rational reason to dwell on negativities from your past. Instead, you should focus on the future and the great things you are going to achieve in the time to come. This is especially true when the insurmountable obstacle does not impact your passions and the purpose of your life.

At what point do you quit? What is your breaking point? Do you give up for the right reasons, at the right time, in the right circumstances?

Doubts, uncertainties or difficult situations or obstacles
Other people's advice to do something else
None of these are reasons to quit
Only quit when you have lost your passion
When you don't like what you are doing anymore
Or when there is really no other alternative
But then find a new passion, a new purpose in life

THE 7-STEP UNIVERSAL SUCCESS CYCLE

Step 1: Desires are the basis of all Success

The starting point of all success lies in the initiation of a desire. Your desires and passions create all the resolve, energy and enthusiasm you need to see your goal through till the end. Success requires commitment and efforts coming from your heart and deepest beliefs, and it is your passion and desires that drive this. A strong desire and passion for something causes a chain reaction.

Step 2: Setting purposeful Goals

Your desire for a certain condition will move you to set a goal. Goals must be sustainable and purposeful. At the highest level, your life's main goal, the reasons for being on earth, the goal must be linked to improving the life of other people. Goals must be based on the principles of ethics, as otherwise they are not sustainable. In order to see your goals through till achievement, you must have a high focus on the goal, never losing it out of your sight, visualising every day how it will be when you attain your goal. You must commit to your goal and have the strong belief that it can be done, and give your goal priority in your daily existence. Write down your goals in every detail with a precise deadline, and soak this in your conscious and subconscious mind every day through visualisation and meditation.

Step 3: Believe in Success

Your belief determines why, how, when and how much of your goals you expect to be realised. A strong belief leads to a high expectation and anticipation of your goal to be achieved. A weak belief causes low expectations for the achievement of your goal. Belief in one's own success is one of the most powerful drivers behind succeeding in what you set out to achieve. Whatever you set out as a goal, you need to believe that it can be done. This belief sets the conscious and subconscious mind in motion to find ways to realise your belief. Develop strong beliefs in your successes and have your mind figure out ways to achieving your goals. Your mind will work hard and will not disappoint you. On the other hand, when you have a conviction that you will fail to achieve your goal, your mind will also work hard not to disappoint your expectations. Success, wealth, good relationships and health do not drop in your lap by just wishing to have them. Intentionally harnessing the power of the law of attraction, focussing the law of attraction on what you want to get from life, will bring you to what you desire. You can eliminate disbelief and strengthen belief in your own success through a disciplined, focused and trained mind. Don't listen to the disbelief of other people. Meditate: every day set aside time to seek silence and become one with your goals. Eliminate self-limiting behaviours and beliefs, as fears and limitations only exist in your mind. Think about what you want; don't think about what you don't want. Use visualisation to strengthen your belief in the achievement of your goals. Have only positive thoughts about success; observe negative thoughts when they arise, but don't give them attention and eliminate them immediately. Don't be concerned with judgment of others, when other people express their disbelief. Look for positive aspects in each event, even when at first glance your mind interprets it as a negative event. You can control what you are thinking about the whole day. Steer your thoughts to believe in success.

Step 4: Consistent and focused Actions

The only right time to start acting on your goals is in the here and now, immediately. You only move closer to your goals when you take action every day. But that action must be ethical, as results achieved by unethical behaviour will not last. There is no need to take something away from another person, as there is enough in the Universe for everyone's success. Hard work might be required to move yourself forward, but hard work alone won't make you wealthy. You need to shift yourself from the competitive field of physical labour to the creative field of mental labour in order to amass wealth. When your product or service advances the life of your customers, they are going to pay you a cash premium in return. It is the accumulation of these cash premiums, coming from many people, which make you wealthy. After being clear on your goal, make a detailed action plan on how to achieve your goal, and consistently execute your plan, day by day. Do each day what you can do to progress towards your goal. Make sure that those actions are efficient and effective. In order to get from where you are today to where you want to be, you have to invest in yourself as well. Embark on a self-improvement programme to increase your level of proficiency through education, training, experience, reading and studying. The better you get at what you do, the easier and quicker you reach your goal.

Step 5: Overcoming Obstacles

It is a matter of fact that obstacles come in your way. These obstacles might be created in your own thinking, rooted in fear for failure; your mind may come up with many excuses why something is not possible. Self-created obstacles don't exist in the real world; they only exist in your mind. They are not real, but will make you delay, postpone or avoid any actions to becoming successful or moving your life forward to a level of joy, satisfaction and happiness not experienced before. You will never experience this when you procrastinate based on your fears. You can overcome these obstacles by controlling your mind. Similarly, negative thinking about future obstacles might freeze you in your tracks. Your mind can run wild about potential future problems that may linger on the horizon. But as long as your current pathway does not indicate that you will come across these obstacles, there is no need to worry about them. Only when you see that you are going to bump into a future obstacle when you don't change course, you need to take action and change the direction. Some obstacles come out of nowhere and cannot be foreseen. They do not seem to be related to any of your activities, rather Fate or Karma has put them on your path. Similar to the other existing obstacles, you can overcome them through persistence in your thinking about success, never admitting to failure, and through persistence in your actions, never quitting. Your persistence is based on the willpower and determination to see your actions through till you reach your goal and you become successful. This, however, requires flexibility as well. Don't be too rigid and glued to old routines when it comes to solving problems or overcoming bad times. With patience, dedication, persistence and the right actions you can overcome all the obstacles on your pathway to success. You can not only overcome them, but even profit from them. There is something positive in each bad situation. Think positive and you will discover the positive side of obstacles. They offer learning and business opportunities if you are willing to see those. It is only the most successful people that come out of a crisis better than they were before the crisis. You don't live alone in this world, and you need the cooperation of other people to realise your dream. As each person has their own dream, you need to carefully manage other people to make them support your goal achievement. You need to be fair, humane, honest and ethical in your dealings with other people, if you want them to follow you and do what you want them to do. Negative people, always complaining and stating why something cannot be done, have no place in your team. Make sure that you surround yourself by people who enable your progression to success, not those who block your way or slow you down.

Step 6: Measuring and reviewing Progress

Determine a good measurement or yardstick for your progression and frequently review your actual status against this. The progression itself enables you to check your status towards the success of reaching your goal. In case your progress is lagging your expectation and detailed action plan, refocus some of the actions and initiate corrective measures. The road to success may be long, 5, 10, 15 years or even decades. Progression means keeping momentum in your actions, always doing everything you can each day to move yourself closer to your goal. When your success timeline is long, you need to keep your focus, even though this may be hard. Always keep your focus on the big prize, and let your passion for what you do drive you to new heights.

Step 7: Achieving Success

Before you are successful, you can already create the appearance of success. You probably have a vision of how you will look like when you achieved your goals. Be that person now already! Today already dress like your vision. Buy the clothing and accessories that match the future you. Carry yourself like a successful person, with the confidence that you have already made it. Other people will think that you are successful and thus treat you like a successful person. This brings you new opportunities, and when you are prepared for them, you become successful. You can never quit, as when you give up, you never realise your goal and all past efforts will have been for nothing. There is only one circumstance creating an exception to this rule. That is when you have lost your passion. When the fire and love for what you are doing has died, reignite that fire and love by refocusing on those aspects of your life where your passion has shifted. When you love what you do, and you do what you love, all efforts will seem easy and naturally to you. When you finally reach your goal, other people will say how lucky you are. But they don't see the hard work and all the efforts you have put into getting there. Luck does not exist; it is the sum of preparation and opportunities. People who are not prepared are not able to create and seize opportunities, and thus fail, often using the term bad luck as an excuse. Your passion for your goal, your persistence, commitment, belief and focus will progress you so far that you have achieved your goal. You have become successful. You need to celebrate your success and share the success with those people who supported you in becoming successful.

Your pathway does not end there. The cycle continues. Once you achieved your goal, you want to set bigger goals. Move yourself, your external conditions and your life to the next level by setting even bigger goals. As long as you still have the desires and passions for what you are doing, keep pushing this cycle of bigger and even bigger goals. Because when you achieve those bigger goals, society, will benefit from your efforts, and you will be increasing improvements for more and more people. The more people you can reach, the bigger your contribution to society.

The 7 Step Universal Success Cycle

When you bring the description of this pathway into one flow chart, it visualises the Universal Success Cycle. This Success Cycle provides concrete and practical guidance to achieve success. It is a standardised and simple formula to get you from where you are today to success in all major aspects in your life. The Success Cycle, when followed, reveals the intense power to achieve success for everyone, everywhere, anytime. Like with achieving any goal in your life, of course, this needs clarity, courage, determination, and persistence. But when you follow through, success will surely come your way. Everybody has the same possibility to become successful. Some people seize the possibilities, others don't. It is not that someone is not successful because there is no possibility to be successful. You are not failing in achieving a rewarding life due to lack of supply of rewards. There are enough rewards available in the Universe. You can have what you desire, realise your dreams and become successful.

Use the Success Cycle as the guiding star in your quest for success. Anyone can be successful, and when you seriously and closely follow the map, it will guide you to success. Guaranteed. But you have to be committed, focused and believe in your success. You must be passionate about what you do, and be focused and give your goal priority in your life. You need to do all you can each day to progress and overcome obstacles through persistence and flexible actions. You need to be prepared and seize opportunities. You need to control your mind to overcome self-created obstacles and manage other people to support you in your quest. You see, it is all up to you. Only you determine whether you will be successful or not. The point is that you can be successful, and that you will be when you follow the 7-Step Universal Success Cycle.

Follow the 7-Step Universal Success Cycle to realise Wealth and Abundance and the Life of your Dreams

Everyone wants to be successful, but not everyone is
There is a certain way of doing things leading to success or non-success
This Universal Success Cycle reveals the certain way that leads to success

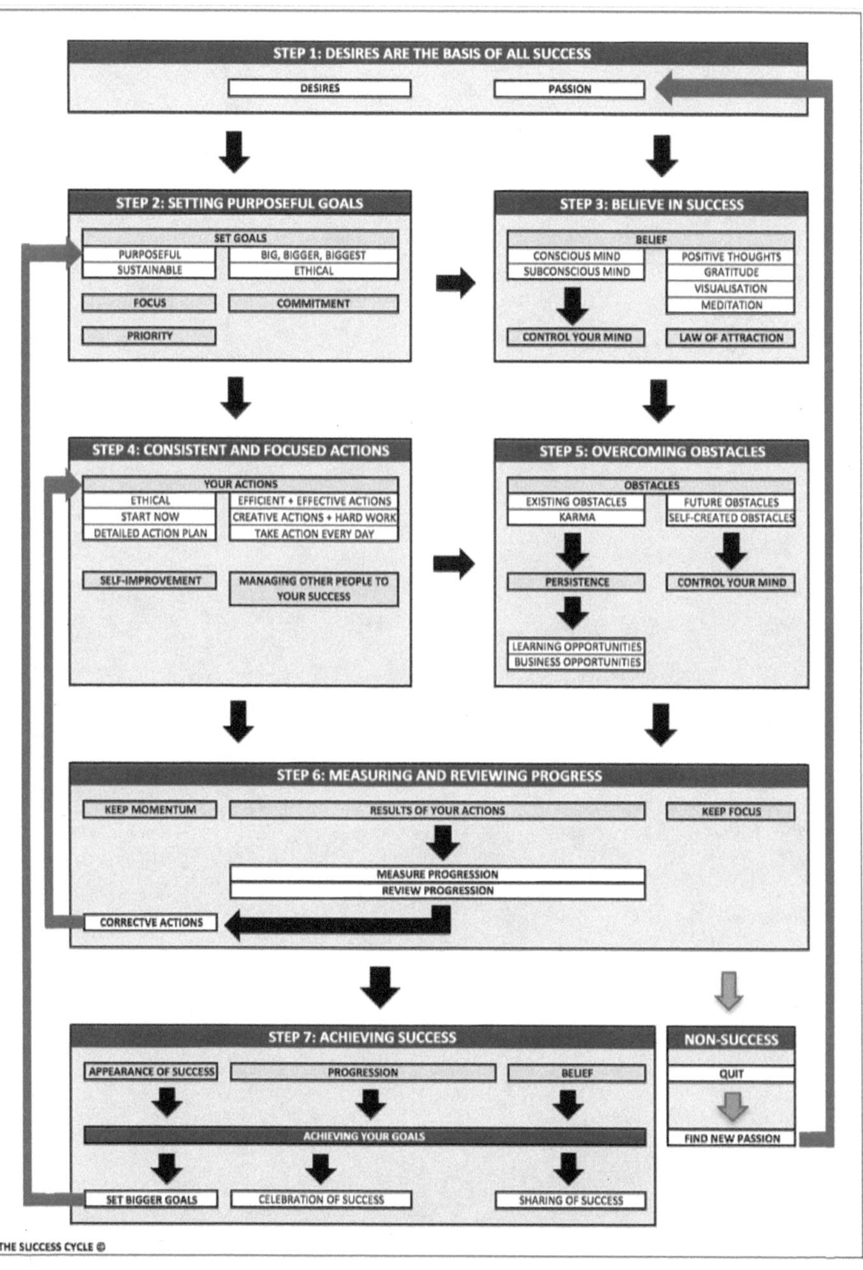
STEP 1: DESIRES ARE THE BASIS OF ALL SUCCESS
DESIRES
PASSION
STEP 2: SETTING PURPOSEFUL GOALS
SET GOALS
PURPOSEFUL
SUSTAINABLE
BIG, BIGGER, BIGGEST
ETHICAL
FOCUS
COMMITMENT
PRIORITY
STEP 3: BELIEVE IN SUCCESS
BELIEF
CONSCIOUS MIND
SUBCONSCIOUS MIND
POSITIVE THOUGHTS
GRATITUDE
VISUALISATION
MEDITATION
CONTROL YOUR MIND
LAW OF ATTRACTION
STEP 4: CONSISTENT AND FOCUSED ACTIONS
YOUR ACTIONS
ETHICAL
START NOW
DETAILED ACTION PLAN
EFFICIENT + EFFECTIVE ACTIONS
CREATIVE ACTIONS + HARD WORK
TAKE ACTION EVERY DAY
SELF-IMPROVEMENT
MANAGING OTHER PEOPLE TO YOUR SUCCESS
STEP 5: OVERCOMING OBSTACLES
OBSTACLES
EXISTING OBSTACLES
KARMA
FUTURE OBSTACLES
SELF-CREATED OBSTACLES
PERSISTENCE
CONTROL YOUR MIND
LEARNING OPPORTUNITIES
BUSINESS OPPORTUNITIES
STEP 6: MEASURING AND REVIEWING PROGRESS
KEEP MOMENTUM
RESULTS OF YOUR ACTIONS
KEEP FOCUS
MEASURE PROGRESSION
REVIEW PROGRESSION
CORRECTVE ACTIONS
STEP 7: ACHIEVING SUCCESS
APPEARANCE OF SUCCESS
PROGRESSION
BELIEF
ACHIEVING YOUR GOALS
SET BIGGER GOALS
CELEBRATION OF SUCCESS
SHARING OF SUCCESS
NON-SUCCESS
QUIT
FIND NEW PASSION
THE SUCCESS CYCLE ©

BIBLIOGRAPHY

Beumer, Hans. *Happiness for Everyone*, Zug: Hans Beumer Publications, 2016

Byrnes, Rhonda. *The secret*, London: Simon & Schuster, 2006.

Canfield, Jack. *Key to living the law of attraction*, Deerfield Beach: Health Communications, 2007

Canfield, Jack. *The success principles: how to get from where you are to where you want to be*, New York: HarperCollins, 2007

Collier, Robert. *The secret of the ages*, New York: Tarcher/Penguin, 2007

Haanel, Charles. *The Master Key System*, St. Louis: Psychology Publishing, 1912

Hill, Napoleon. *Think and grow rich*, New York: Tarcher/Penguin, 2005

Schwartz, David J. *The magic of thinking big*, New York: Simon & Schuster, 2012

Trump, Donald and Zanker, Bill. *Thinking Big, make it happen in Business and Life*, New York: Harper, 2007

Taylor, Sandra Anne. *Quantum Success*, Carlsbad: Hay House, 2007

Wattles, Wallace. *The Science Of Getting Rich*, New York: Elizabeth Towne Publishing, 1910

ABOUT THE AUTHOR

drs. Hans Beumer is an enthusiastic and seasoned traveller and a passionate Author. He has travelled all over the world, exploring many different cultures.

Throughout his working life Hans has always been very analytical and he fine-tuned his skills to present complex and difficult topics in a simple and transparent way. This enables him to take the difficult to grasp abstract and philosophical concepts such as Happiness and Success, and analyse and present them in easy to understand way. This analytical approach separates him from the herd of other writers producing books on the same topics. Hans's approach makes the topics easily accessible and understandable for the larger audience.

As an Author he shares his experiences with the world. His books are the carrying vehicles of his passion, and their publishing enables him to reach and touch the life of many millions of other people on all continents. It is his aim to increase the level of happiness in the world.

The Author wrote this book while being in Switzerland, Hawaii and Spain.

Contact information:
Please visit www.hansbeumer.com

www.ingramcontent.com/pod-product-compliance
Lightning Source LLC
LaVergne TN
LVHW090957080826
845145LV00003B/1035

* 9 7 8 3 9 0 6 8 6 1 1 1 1 *

The Lawman's Mail Order Bride

Mail-Order Brides of Sweet, Texas, Book One

Mail-Order Brides of Sweet, Texas, historically inspired clean and wholesome romance.

Hold onto your bonnets you're about to meet the biggest matchmaking cupid of the west…

Mail Order Bride Lucy Calvert's nerves rattled as she stepped off the stagecoach in Sweet, Texas. She'd traveled from St. Louis to meet her betrothed, the sheriff of the tiny town. Nervous and excited to meet Trey Jones and his small daughter, she's dismayed when he's not there to meet her. Shocked even more when the older, giant of a man, Big John Wiggins takes her bag and takes her to meet him. But the biggest shock is to find out that Trey did not send for a mail-order bride…but if not him, then who did she correspond too?

Who sent for her in the lawman's name?

There's a mystery in the tiny town of Sweet when mail-order brides begin to show up for the men one at a time and the town wonders who sent for them. The brides and the grooms wonder more.

Watching them work out the situation is the fun part.

At least it is for Big John Wiggins a widower who knows the joys of a happy marriage and the six foot, five inch widower has decided the men of his town need wives and joy too. Even if it takes him to bring the women to them.

CHAPTER ONE

Big John Wiggins stood in the doorway of his feed store and watched as the stagecoach rolled into Sweet, Texas. He crossed his big arms and grinned in anticipation—would today be the day when Lucy Calvert arrived? If his plan worked, fun and more'n likely, fireworks, were about to start in his boring little town. He loved this dusty little place, where he and his sweet wife, rest her soul, had settled ten years ago. It was struggling and he wanted it to succeed, but a town without families stagnated and it seemed that was what was happening with Sweet.

He'd decided to take things into his own hands-to stir the pot, as his Millie used to say. The town had plenty of cowboys and plowboys spread out all over the area. But like many frontier towns, there was a shortage of women. And that wasn't good.

They needed wives.

Big John had seen one too many cowboys dragging into his feed store, looking like lonesome hound dogs and he couldn't take it any longer.

Finally, he'd decided something had to be done.

And that was when he'd taken matters into his own hands and written a few letters. Miss Calvert was the first mail-order bride to agree to come. And any day now she should be showing up on the stagecoach. It could be today, if so life was about to get interesting.

Yes sir, fireworks were about to start and he was going to sit back and watch them go off. And pray. He'd decided not to let on that he was the instigator…that might be wrong, but he had a longterm plan and people didn't need to know. Knowing could mess it all up.

When he'd decided to send letters, a few months

ago, to the premier mail-order-bride catalog in St. Louis, Miss Adaline Bingham's Mail-Order Bride Agency he'd been committed to see this through. He'd gone through Miss Bingham because she had a good reputation and vouched for the women she represented as honest women looking for a fresh start in the West.

He was acting as the voucher for the men of Sweet and had chosen each man carefully. Men he believed needed a wife the most and would be good to a wife.

Sheriff Trey Jones was top of the list.

He was a widower whose little girl needed a mother. Big John had found the perfect little lady for Trey and corresponded with her in Trey's name.

Guilt hit him. But Big John pushed it away for the greater good he could do. Misleading the young woman and the surprise that she and Trey would have when she showed up, didn't sit well with him. But he felt in his heart it would be worth it. He saw a need and he was fixing it. Of course, if things didn't work out the way they should, then he'd step in and own up to his part everything. He would always be watching, hovering like the young woman's protector.

The good Lord willing, he would be able to match the mail-order brides up with the perfect lonesome cowboy and they'd enjoy a wonderful life together, like he had with his Millie for thirty-seven years before he'd lost her to the fever.

These cowboys might not know what was good for them at first but he figured they'd come around, one pretty little lady at a time.

The stagecoach door opened. A small hand reached out and took the driver's and then a young lady, dressed in a lavender dress, stepped from the stagecoach and into Big John's sight.

Blonde curls, bright blue eyes, and a pert mouth, Miss Lucy Calvert was just as pretty as the picture she had included with her first letter.

Yep, things in Sweet were about to get interesting.

Lucy Calvert's nerves rattled around inside her as much as the stagecoach had rattled across Texas. Her heart thundered in her chest like a foghorn from one of the riverboats that floated down the Mississippi back home in St. Louis as she stepped onto the boarded sidewalk of the town she was about to call home. Lucy's stomach knotted and she fought wanting to get back in the stagecoach to go back home.

But she couldn't do that. She had no desire to go back to St. Louis.

She looked around the small town, with its clapboard buildings, the small church at the end of the street. And as far as she could see, there was an array of stores…more than just the saloon on the corner. Her gaze caught on the two older ladies standing outside the general store on the far side of the street. They were watching her with curiosity. She was happy to note that there were some other women in town. A tall, thin man was sweeping the sidewalk in front of the store and stopped to look her way. Two cowboys riding by on horses slowed and tipped their hats at her. Men drove by in wagons. Some men came out of the saloon. Men stood not too terribly far away from her, leaning against porch posts. There were men everywhere!

There just wasn't one waiting for her to get off the

stagecoach.

Heart fluttering, she glanced at the very large man inside the doorway of the feed store where the stagecoach had stopped. He smiled a welcoming smile. She smiled back at the jovial stranger.

The stagecoach driver dropped her baggage from the roof and lugged her chest off the back side of the coach and then came back to her. "Well, little miss, I guess that's it. It was a pleasure."

"Thank you so much for getting me here safely. I'm forever in your debt."

The old rough-edged stagecoach driver scratched his grizzly beard, his eyes skeptical. "You sure you're gonna be okay here? I don't see no man here to meet you, ma'am."

"Thank you for your concern but I'm sure he'll be here soon. He's the sheriff so something may have delayed him."

"Okay, then I've got places to be. I wish you luck." He climbed back up into the seat, grumbling as he went.

"Excuse me," Lucy said, thinking she had

misunderstood what he grumbled. "What did you say?"

He looked sheepishly down at her. "I said, all these mail-order brides coming out here meetin' up with all these fellas that they never seen before—its jest disturbin'. I've seen a few broken hearts and I've taken a many back the way they came."

"But how did you know I was a mail-order bride?" She was shocked because she hadn't said a word about that.

"I recognized it in yor eyes and in the way you got off that stage. You have an expectant, uncertain look about you. I'm jest going to wish you the best." He tipped his hat and spat a stream of tobacco, making her cringe.

Her stomach trembled as she watched the stagecoach rumble away. The flying dust made her cough. She waved her hand in front of her face to get rid of the dust and looked around.

Where was Trey Jones?

He had said he was the sheriff in town. She hadn't wanted to admit it to the old stagecoach driver but you would think the sheriff would be here to meet her.

"Miss. Can I help you?"

She turned to find the man from the feed store smiling at her.

"I'm John Wiggins. Everyone calls me Big John."

"Hello, I'm Lucy Calvert and I'm looking for Sheriff Trey Jones. Could you tell me the direction of the sheriff's office, please?"

"Yes, ma'am, indeed I can. If you walk right down there, past the general store, past the alley, the jailhouse is around the corner." He paused. "You can't miss it. It's got a big sign on it that says Sheriff's Office."

Was it her imagination or did this guy act as though he found this amusing? This was very curious. "Thank you, sir. I can't carry my valise all the way down there. It weighs a lot. Could you store it inside your store for me, along with my trunk? Just for a little while?"

He grinned. "I'll do better than that. I'll escort you down to the sheriff's office and carry your valise for you."

"That would be very kind of you and very appreciated."

He walked over to her trunk, picked it up and hauled it into his store. He pulled his door closed and then picked up her bag. He hitched a brow at her. "What do you have in here? Rocks?" He chuckled.

She liked him. "That's one thing I forgot to put in there."

He laughed. "Well, I'm glad about that or I might not be able to carry it. Let's go find the sheriff."

Lucy felt relieved to have the big man beside her as she walked down the street toward her future husband.

Trey Jones was thumbing through the wanted posters. He tried to keep a lookout as best he could. There weren't any of these bad characters running around his town but unsavory fellows seemed to ramble in from time to time, and he liked to keep his mind refreshed on their faces so he'd recognize them if he saw them.

When the door opened and Big John stepped in, he

was glad for a break. "Big John, what brings you and—" His words halted as a pretty young woman in a dusty, lavender dress stepped inside the door Big John held open for her and her big blue gaze met his.

He shot up out of his chair. "Ma'am." He looked from her to Big John and then back to her. "Can I help you?"

Big John rubbed his neck and looked slightly uncomfortable. "This little lady got off the stagecoach a few minutes ago with this big bag and she couldn't bring it all the way down here so I carried it for her."

That pretty young woman clasped her small hands together and rocked back on her feet as if nervous, making her dress swing forward and then back like a bell swinging. "I came from St. Louis. I'm Lucy Calvert."

Trey got the feeling that he was supposed to react to her name. As if she expected him to know who she was. "I'm Trey Jones, the sheriff of Sweet. Do you have a problem, Miss Calvert?"

She looked confused. "No, I don't have a problem. I'm here to meet you. I came all this way and thought you would meet me at the stagecoach."

"Meet you?" His brows knit together and he looked at Big John, who hitched a brow and looked slightly amused. "I'm not sure I understand. Did something happen on the stagecoach and you needed a lawman?"

"No, nothing *happened*." She looked startled again. Her gaze cut to Big John and then back to him. "I thought you'd meet me since I came all this way to marry you."

Trey froze. *What?* "What did you say? You came to *marry* me?"

She nodded slowly as color drained from her face. "You sent for me," she said, softly.

Alarm raked over him like burning coals. "What do you mean, I sent for you?" he croaked.

"At Miss Adaline Bingham's Mail-Order Bride Agency."

Mail-order bride. Trey swallowed, trying hard to dislodge the hundred-pound frog that clogged his throat. A thought flashed through him that he and his daughter, Janie, could use a woman in their life…but he hadn't sent for a mail-order bride.

"You didn't send for me?" Disappointment flooded her face.

"No, ma'am…I mean," he fumbled and shot a plea for help at Big John. The feed store owner shrugged. He looked back at her. "I didn't send a letter for a wife."

Her eyes filled with tears.

She going to cry? That was the last thing he needed. He moved around the corner of the desk. *Was he about to have a hysterical female on his hands?* He couldn't abide a crying woman. Didn't know what to do with them. He'd hated when his Beth had cried and he'd felt helpless. As he did now. A crying woman always took him back to his childhood when his mother cried a lot after his dad had been killed in the war. It had been a hard time for a boy struggling with his own grief.

He reached out and touched Miss Calvert's arm, hoping to give her comfort. He felt her arm tense at his touch and he looked to Big John. "What should I do?"

Big John looked sympathetic. "Well, you could

give it a thought maybe—I mean, it looks like somebody in town thought you needed a wife and sent for one for you. Maybe you could consider it."

He glared at Big John. *Had he lost his mind?*

Disbelief rolled over him like a herd of buffalo charging across the prairie. *Marry*? He wasn't thinking about marriage! After Beth had died, something in him had died too and he didn't know whether he could ever marry again. Although, guilt hit him. Janie sure did need a woman's touch. She was growing up far too fast and would blossom into a young woman before he blinked. At six years old, she had a mind of her own and thought she could stay at home alone around the corner at their house. If it hadn't been for the church quilting club, the older ladies in town who'd stepped up to help him out when Janie was born and left without a mother, then he would have been in trouble. But Miss Clara, Miss Essie Jane Tate and Mrs. Mulberry, to name a few, had stepped in to help. *He and Janie were making it...*

He didn't need to marry. *Did he?*

Anger and disbelief came over him again. *Who*

would have sent for a bride for him?

His mind began to roll around, thinking about who all might've done this and immediately the quilters came to mind. *Would they have done it?*

Mrs. Mulberry had told him the last time he had to load up and lead a posse out of town that maybe he needed to be thinking more about Janie than the town because she would be alone in the world if he got himself killed out there looking for outlaws.

He thought about that now. *Did he need to think about Janie?* Guilt jabbed at him.

"I think maybe we need to get you set up over at Miss Clara's boardinghouse. We can think more clearly about this after some rest. Maybe you can get back on that stagecoach when he comes back through and go back home. There isn't much else I can do for you."

"But I just don't understand. I don't have any place to go back to. I sent you two letters, and you replied that you were happy for me to come. You even sounded excited! You said little Janie and I would get along well and with my teaching ability, that it would be a good thing. I just don't understand."

Who had done this? He found that question floating in his mind but looking into her blue eyes and seeing the worry there and the fact that she had no place to go back to worried him. But that wasn't what had his attention; it was those big blue eyes of hers. They glared at him. Beth had big blue eyes that peered at him the same way when she wanted something and she knew how to use those eyes. It had been a long time since he had thought about blue eyes.

"Are you going to send me back?"

"No. But we'll go to Miss Clara's and get you a room for the night. I'll pay for it for a few days until we get this straightened out."

"From my point of view, I think you need to be thinking about the wife part," Big John said, skeptically. "Don't you at least need a housekeeper? Or someone to keep Janie company? Instead of paying room and board for her over at Miss Clara's, maybe you could hire her on as your housekeeper for a while?"

Big John was a wise man. Everyone in town

respected his opinion as a pillar of the community and yes, he was right. Trey actually could use help. "But I don't know her. How do I know she can be trusted with my daughter?"

"You're the lawman, Trey. Look at this woman and tell me you think that she's a bad person. You've got good instincts."

Trey sighed. It was true—he did have good instincts. He was just trying to find his way right now. "Okay, maybe after you stay at Miss Clara's for the night, so I can break this to Janie, then maybe I can consider me hiring you to help take care of my daughter. And to take care of my household."

"I, I guess that will be fine. But I came here to be a bride. I have hopes of…" She looked from one man to the other. A rose blush colored her skin. "I would love to have a family of my own one day and that's why I came out here."

Something in his stomach got all nervous and funny feeling. "I won't be stopping you from that. There's a lot of single men in this town."

Big John grinned. "This could be your lucky day,

little lady. You can meet a man of your own choosing instead of coming out here not really knowing who you're going to marry."

She looked uncertain but her eyes grew bright as she thought about what Big John said.

Trey realized he really hoped the best for her and he said so. "I really think this is the best thing for you."

Hope filled her eyes. "Okay, I'll do it."

"Fine, then we're all set. Let's go to Miss Clara's." He moved toward the door.

Big John stepped back and let him lead her outside. Samuel Donavan, his deputy, rode up as Big John closed the door. The younger man dismounted from his horse and tied it to the hitching post as he looked curiously at Lucy.

"Ma'am." He tipped his hat and smiled at the young woman. "Samuel Donavan, deputy of Sweet," he gushed.

Big John grinned. "Samuel, this is Miss Lucy Calvert. She's new in town."

"That's wonderful news." Samuel looked like a puppy needing a belly rub.

Lucy smiled back at his deputy and Trey's mood darkened. "Maybe we need to head on over to Miss Clara's. Samuel, watch the office while I'm gone."

"Sure." The deputy grinned at Miss Calvert. "It's nice to meet you, miss."

Trey took Miss Calvert's arm and hustled her down the sidewalk. He'd get her settled in and then go from there. One thing he didn't want right now was all these fellows in town thinking that just because she was here they suddenly had rights to her.

What was he thinking that for? He didn't have rights to her either. *Did he?*

CHAPTER TWO

Lucy felt dazed by the things that had happened since she'd gotten off the stagecoach. This wasn't the way it was supposed to happen. The sheriff—she didn't even know how to address the man she'd thought would be her husband.

People watched them as they paraded down the street. She felt very self-conscious walking beside the sheriff. They made their way down the street that led to the boardinghouse just around the corner and a short walk down a side street. He was rigid and just as stunned as she was at learning she had come to marry him. The only difference in their situations was that she had communicated with someone. To think that she had been communicating with someone who was pretending to be Trey Jones. She'd had two letters from him and she'd responded. But to whom?

The boardinghouse was a two-story white house with a large front porch enclosed by a porch railing. And her heart dropped when she saw the cats sitting on the railing. One was curled in a wicker chair and several sat on the porch. There were two chairs sitting beside a little table. Lucy didn't do well with cats. But at this point, she was hesitant to say anything.

Maybe the cats would stay away. But as they walked up the steps, three curious cats moved toward them. As he knocked on the door, one of them came and rubbed against her dress! She sidestepped, but it rolled to its side. She tried to get out of its way without anyone noticing. The cat rolled beneath her skirt and she fought not to gasp. The screen door opened and a plump woman in her sixties smiled at them. Lucy tried to focus on the rosy-cheeked lady while at the same time she gently nudged the cat with the toe of her foot. The cat rubbed against her leg.

Oh dear goodness, this was not good.

"Well, hello, Sheriff. How can I help you today?" Miss Clara asked, pleasantly.

Lucy shook her leg and tried not to cringe.

"Miss Clara, it's nice to see you today. This is Miss Lucy Calvert. She's just gotten off the stagecoach and is in need of a place to stay tonight, and maybe tomorrow night."

"It's so nice to meet you. Yes, dear, I have a lovely room for you. Please come in." She backed up, giving them room to enter. Two cats ran out of the house.

Lucy's throat began to itch as she stepped into the house and away from the cat under her dress. Immediately, however, her stomach dipped when she saw two pretty white cats sitting on the back of the couch, and a calico and a black cat sitting on the cushion of a chair.

Her skin began to itch more. She closed her eyes

and willed her reaction to go away.

Miss Clara walked into the room, talking pleasantly, and Trey relaxed slightly.

"Your room is upstairs, first one on the right. I hope you don't mind my cats. I just love cats. They're such creative little critters and since my husband passed away, I have just enjoyed their company."

"Lovely." Lucy voice sounded hoarse.

Trey glanced at her. Her eyes were puffy and her skin was becoming red and splotchy. Alarm rang through him.

"Oh dear," Miss Clara gasped.

"Are you you—" he started to ask but suddenly Lucy clutched her throat and her knees buckled.

"Can't breathe," she gasped as she stumbled forward into Trey's arms. "Cats—"

"We need to get her outside. Now," Big John demanded.

Trey was already lifting her into his arms. He moved through the door Big John held open and kept walking until he was out in the middle of the yard into the fresh air, away from the cats.

"Maybe you should take her to the doctor," Miss Clara exclaimed, wringing her hands.

"Can you breathe now?" Trey stared into her eyes. His heart raced with worry as she sucked in fresh air and nodded. Relief filled him. "Has this happened before?"

"Yes, but only with cats," she managed. "I don't need a doctor. I'll be fine after I get this fresh air and take a bath. That helps with the itching."

Trey contemplated what to do.

"Maybe we need to take her back to your place for now," Big John said. "I mean, at least so that the poor woman can relax for a minute and you've got a tub."

Trey slammed him with a hard stare.

"Well, she needs a bath, Trey."

Trey rubbed his temple. "Okay, you're right. Can you walk?" It wasn't her fault that they were in this fix. It was the person who'd played this dirty trick on them. He steadied her.

"Yes, I'm fine. Just itching now."

“Oh good.” Miss Clara looked relieved. “I am so sorry about the kitties.”

“Thank you so much for trying to accommodate me. My allergy is not your fault. Your cats are adorable. I wish I wasn’t allergic to them so I could pet them.”

“Aw,” Miss Clara cooed. “You are so sweet. I’d hug you but then I’ve been holding my little darlings and might make you break out worse.”

“Thank you, I might indeed. Still, it’s a nice thought.”

“You take her to your house and take good care of her, Sheriff.”

Trey found himself mesmerized by Lucy’s sweet smile and attitude. “I will. Let’s get going. You’ll feel better after you freshen up and relax a little while.”

“Thank you. I don’t mean to be a bother but that would be best.”

Trey nodded, dreading the long walk through town toward his home. He cupped her elbow, assisting her along the rough road onto the sidewalk when they reached Main Street. Big John followed them, carrying her bags.

Everyone stopped to stare.

Feeling self-conscious and out of his element, Trey stalked down the street, trying to hurry Lucy to his home.

What would Janie think? He wasn't sure but it couldn't be helped. Yes, there were other widows he could put Lucy up with but the poor woman had been through enough right now.

They walked up to his small house on the side street, not too far from the sheriff's office. He bought the little house just for that reason—that it was fairly close to the office. If need be, he could just run around the corner to check on Janie when she was home alone. Also, Janie could come get him if she needed to. Everybody in town knew little Janie and he knew he could count on those good people to look out for her. But Janie was weary of being shuffled around from one helpful widow after the other. Mrs. Mulberry was the most helpful but he'd begun to feel bad that Janie spent more time with the older woman or alone than she did with him.

He ran a hand through his hair. His life was in a pickle, a big pickle, and now it was in worse shape than before. His stomach was turning hollow, as if he hadn't eaten in days. He stepped up on his front porch, keeping his hand on Lucy's elbow. She seemed to be better but she was still pink and splotchy and seemed out of breath. Maybe he had hurried too fast down the street.

Again, guilt prodded him.

Before he could open the door, it flew open and there stood Janie. Her braided pigtails were lopsided and lumpy but she was his pride and joy. It wasn't her fault that he couldn't braid worth dirt and she still struggled with how to do it herself.

He wished that she had gone to Mrs. Mulberry's today or Miss Essie Jane Tate's but she had wanted to stay home and play in her room. She seemed content to play in her room a lot these days.

"Who are you?" Janie then looked real close. "What's wrong with your skin?"

Out of the mouths of babes. There was one thing Trey had learned since becoming a father and it was that you never knew what a kid was going to say.

Especially Janie.

"Now Janie, don't be rude."

"Sorry, Pa. Ma'am, I didn't mean to be rude but you look terrible. Like I did when I got in poison oak last year. Do you itch? I itched something terrible."

"Well, actually I do—"

"I'll get you a cool wet rag. It made mine feel better."

"Let's get you inside, Lucy. You can sit down and rest." He led the way inside.

Big John set the suitcases on the floor just inside the room. "Well now, I'm going to leave you two and go back to check on my store. Hope you get this worked out. If either of you need anything, just give me a holler. I'm just a stone throw away. But you two are nice adults and I feel you all can get this straightened out yourselves. Miss Lucy, it's been a pleasure meeting you. And like I said, if you need anything, my store is a short walk from here and I'm at your service."

With that, Big John backed out the door and shot

Trey a warning look that said he better watch himself and take care of the little woman or he'd be reckoned with. Trey understood the look. Big John was a protective fella—always had been. But still, the warning shot irritated Trey. He hadn't done anything wrong. And he was the sheriff, by gosh.

Lucy ignored the two men and smiled at the blunt, but adorable, little girl studying her intently. "I would love a cold rag if you could get me one."

"I'll be right back." Janie spun and raced out of the room.

"Let's get you sitting down," Trey said.

She tried to think of him as the sheriff but, even though she'd learned that he wasn't who she had been communicating with, she still kept thinking of him as her soon-to-be husband. But he wasn't. She pushed that from her thoughts and moved to the sofa and was suddenly very aware that they were alone in the room. As she settled on the cushion, she met his troubled gaze.

"Janie, honey, are you getting that cold rag?"

"Coming, Pa. Be right there. I'm pumping the water into the basin."

Lucy tried not to scratch her neck and tried to put herself in his place. He hadn't sent for a mail-order bride and yet he was being so helpful. He was as nice as she'd thought he was in the two letters that he'd told her about himself and Janie. It was hard to realize that he hadn't written those notes, but obvious that the person who had written them knew him…and thought well of him.

So had they known that he needed a wife despite him not realizing it or wanting a wife?

Lucy met his gaze and a shiver raced through her. Quickly she looked away, startled by the way her pulse quickened.

Lucy was already mortified by the situation she found herself in and now, finding herself attracted to the man she'd come to marry was confusing. It would have been a most wonderful feeling if things had turned out as she'd expected when she departed the stagecoach. But now, she wasn't sure what to think.

And the sweet, darling little girl whose new mother she had come all this way to become tugged at her heartstrings. Outspoken but helpful Janie obviously could use a woman's touch. Her hair was a mess and her dress needed the hem let out and the shoulders seams loosened to accommodate for her growth. But even as rumpled as the child was, Lucy was certain she herself looked far worse; with her red and whelped skin, she had to look terrible. Lucy had seen herself in mirrors on other occasions when this had happened…it wasn't a pretty sight.

It was so embarrassing. She rubbed her temple and tried to force a brave front. She could not let this get her down. She had sworn when she got on that stagecoach that she was going to think positive and find a way to make her new life a good one.

The excitement she'd felt at leaving behind the city and coming to the frontier had not distinguished. She had been determined that she would be brave, fearless, and an adventurer. Her aunt had advised her to marry a storekeeper in St. Louis but she'd chosen her own path and now she was going to have to make the most of it.

And she would. Her spirits boosted and her determination reinforced, she lifted her chin and met Trey's uncertain gaze. He really had lovely eyes, such a beautiful color of golds and browns. The distraction of them caused her thoughts to jumble. She knew she looked a fright but there was nothing she could do about that.

She forced herself to speak. "Since we have such a questionable situation—" she started to say just as little Janie came back into the room with a small basin that she sat on the table beside the sofa.

"I'll be right back." She raced out of the room.

"Do you need help?" Trey called.

"No, I've got it, Pa," she yelled in her small voice and then reappeared with a jug. She carried it to the basin and proudly poured the water into the basin. She grinned. "I decided you might need a lot of water. You've got a lot of red spots."

Lucy knew then that her face must really be a sight. The child returned, waving a rag, and handed it to her. “This will make you feel better. Won’t it, Pa?”

“I hope so,” Trey said, looking uncomfortable.

Lucy dipped the rag into the water, wrung it out and then pressed the cloth to her heated skin. She almost sighed in relief.

Trey disappeared and returned with a glass of water. “This might help too.” He held the glass out to her.

She took it. Their fingers touched and butterflies fluttered up her arm and her stomach. Trying not to appear shaken, she took a sip of water as both Trey and Janie watched.

The water soothed her throat. *Oh, what she would do for a bath.* It had been such a long and dusty ride over the last several days; she must be a mess even before becoming a red splotchy disaster.

“You’re pretty, if we had those pink spots off of you.” Janie smiled and touched one of the splotches on Lucy’s hand. “It’s hot. Does it hurt?”

The sweet smile that the little girl gave her touched Lucy’s heart again. From what she had gathered from the letters—that had not actually been from Janie's pa—was that Janie's mother had passed away when Janie was born and that she never had a mother. That had been one of the reasons that Trey's letter had touched her so quickly. Not that it had been from Trey, she reminded herself again; it had been from some stranger. Some person who she had no idea about.

Who would do such a thing?

Clearing her mind, she focused on Janie. "It just itches. This cool rag will help immensely. Thank you so much for this. Are you having a good time today?" She dipped the rag back into the basin and bathed her neck and face for the second time. It felt wonderful.

Janie looked at her shyly now. "I'm having a regular day. I been playing with my doll in my room. Me and my doll wait here for my pa while he's at work, and we fix him sandwiches sometimes. If we've got bread. Mrs. Mulberry and the other nice ladies in town bring us bread when they make some. One day I'll learn so I can make our bread. The ladies in town say that Pa is a strong man and he needs good food to keep him filled out."

Trey frowned and Lucy could not help but admire the way he was filled out.

"I'm glad you're here. You coming here today is making it a really good day." The child rambled on and Lucy couldn't help think that the child sounded lonely.

Trey looked perplexed or maybe even embarrassed and she wondered whether he had just had the same thought, that his child was lonesome.

Lucy met his gaze and anger swelled inside her. This was not right…and suddenly she wondered whether the person who had written the letters also thought this wasn't right.

He truly did need a wife—if not for himself, then for his daughter.

"Janie, you're leading Miss Calvert to think you don't enjoy your life or that you're lonesome all the time. You know we go and do picnics and other outdoor things when I don't work."

"I do enjoy my life, Pa. But she asked me if I was

having a good day and I've been real lonesome today, Pa."

He sighed and rubbed his temple as if warding off a headache. "Janie, why don't you go into your room and play for a while. I need to talk to Miss Calvert alone for a few minutes."

"Okay, but don't leave," Janie warned, looking expectantly at Lucy.

"I won't," Lucy said, feeling awkward as she found herself alone with Trey.

He cleared his throat. "I'm not sure who thought to play this prank on you and me, but it's put us both in an awkward position. However, maybe we can make the most of it. I do need help with the house and Janie, as you can see."

It wasn't what she'd hoped for but it was all she had at the moment. "She's a lovely child. I'll take good care of her."

"I believe that. So, I'll get the water heating on the stove for you to have a warm bath. It'll help you feel better. I'll be home later for supper and we'll get things worked out."

"Thank you. I'll fix dinner."

He looked startled and then smiled. "Okay, that sounds good. Real good. I might get used to this."

He left then, and she sighed, wishing things had been different.

CHAPTER THREE

Trey headed back to his office. He needed to get away. He needed to hide. He needed to figure out who had done this.

Yes, it might end up working out just fine. After all, he would admit that he needed a housekeeper. Somebody to watch after little Janie. But did he need a wife? He didn't think so—he'd had one. And it hurt too much to lose one. He didn't figure he could go through that again unless…unless he married strictly as a matter of getting his daughter a mother.

The thought struck him hard.

Could he do that? He could handle having a housekeeper but would that fill the hole in Janie's heart? Could he marry for her?

He scratched his neck, lost in thought over that as he stepped up onto the plank sidewalk and headed toward the sheriff's office. There was a commotion going on at Big John's. A crowd was gathered there and spilling out onto the sidewalk. Trey decided he better go check that out.

He pushed past the two men blocking the door and into the store.

"Samuel, what's going on here?" he asked his deputy, looking around the crowd of about ten men. He'd spied several of them at the lumber store earlier, loading up their buck wagons and now here they were squeezed in tight at Big John's feed store.

Big John chuckled. "Well, that's simple. Everybody wants to know about your…er, *housekeeper*."

"Yeah," Samuel agreed. "We're just curious. We never seen anybody send off for a *housekeeper* by stagecoach. We were thinking you might have got yourself a mail-order bride."

"And she sure is pretty," someone said, but Trey didn't see who it was because he was trying to figure out what to say to Samuel.

"She's a dainty little thing too." Jeb Brewster spat a stream of tobacco onto the floor and grinned a tobacco-stained grin. "I got me a hankering to send off fer a mail-order bride."

Trey scowled as laughter moved about the room. "She's my housekeeper. She's going to look after little Janie."

"Whatever you say, Sheriff Trey." Horace Holcomb chuckled.

Trey's face twisted and hardened to a scowl that he could feel all the way to the back of his scalp. "Now you listen up," he demanded. "I will not be tolerating you all making snide remarks behind Lucy's back. She's a very nice lady."

"Sorry," Horace muttered.

"Lucy, is it?" Chauncey Todd speculated. The old miner's wrinkled face crinkled up tight. "Them's awful friendly terms you're on with yer housekeeper. And I ain't bein' disrespectful."

Trey looked at Big John, hoping for help.

The feed store owner shrugged. "I tried to tell them you hired her on as a housekeeper. Told them little Janie was real excited. But, as you can see, sometimes it's hard to convince people to change their first impressions."

"I better not hear any snide remarks," he warned. "Or I might have to haul y'all to the jailhouse." He was not feeling too humorous right now.

"Serious?" Samuel asked, his eyes wide with disbelief.

Trey shot him a point-blank stare. "Yes. And if you continue to egg this on, you might be the first one to spend the night in there, *Deputy.*"

"I wouldn't," Samuel muttered. "I thought she was real nice. I'm jealous. It'd be nice to have more young ladies in town."

"Yeah, you don't have to get so testy," Horace said as Samuel clamped his mouth shut tight. "We ain't done nothing but show curiosity. But there aren't many younger women around here."

He realized he was overreacting and soon headed back down the street to his office.

He spotted two ladies from the church quilting club. They were staring at him and chattering as fast as they could talk. Mrs. Mulberry and Miss Essie Jane Tate.

Could they have been the ones who ordered a mail-order bride for him?

They were God-fearing, God-loving…okay, *nosy* women but surely they wouldn't do such a thing…would they?

Lucy was so thankful that Trey had been considerate enough to warm the water and suggest she take a bath to try to feel better. After the long and dusty stagecoach ride and then the cat encounter, she more than welcomed sinking down into the warm water.

After she'd been in the water for a few minutes, Janie looked around the corner at her. "Can I come in?"

“Yes.” She soaped up with the bar of lavender soap she’d pulled out of her bag. That precious bar of soap had traveled all the way from St. Louis with her. She was very grateful that she had packed it.

“I just can’t believe Pa really hired you to be my housekeeper and look after me.” The excitement radiated off the child.

“I’m glad to be here. We will have fun.”

“I think it’s just wonderful. I never had a play friend or housekeeper.” Her brow crinkled. “What exactly does a housekeeper do?”

Lucy chuckled and felt a stab of regret that she wasn’t able to tell Janie that she was going to be her new mother. “It means that I’ll keep the house clean and I’ll do some cooking and I’ll be here for you.” And she would. Something in Janie’s expression was wistful, longing and she wondered whether it came from her longing to have a mother. Lucy knew that feeling. She’d had her aunt but had lost her mother early and had always longed for the closeness that she’d felt. Her aunt had tried, but she’d never been the type a child could cuddle up with in a chair or feel extraordinarily loved by. Looking at Janie, Lucy wished Trey had truly written those letters and had asked her to come here and marry him.

"Can you read me stories before I go to sleep at night?" Janie's expression lit with hope.

"We'll talk to your pa about it and see what he says." She really had no idea how the evenings would be. They hadn't gotten to that far on how they were going to deal with this new situation. There were so many unanswered questions. "Let me get out of the bath and then we'll make supper. How does that sound?"

"Great. I've been wanting to learn to cook."

Lucy's spirits lifted. At least Janie was thrilled that she was here. And for that she was grateful.

By the time Trey called it a day, the sun was hanging low on the horizon. It wasn't his night to make rounds but he'd told Samuel to take the night off. He had decided that tonight he needed an excuse to get out of his house after dinner.

He had the uncomfortable situation of settling his new housekeeper into his home. He felt very uncomfortable about the whole situation. He needed to move his stuff out of his room and into the back storeroom of the house. He'd have to add on sooner than later if this worked out. He felt nervous as he reached his house. He hesitated outside the door into the kitchen and removed his hat. He raked a hand through this hair and realized he needed to get a haircut.

When he walked into the house, his stomach cried out in joy at the delicious scents that filled his home. It was heavenly and his mouth instantly watered. He could hear Janie talking excitedly and Lucy's soft voice. Hearing Janie's happy voice and laughter sent a jolt of happiness through him. He entered the kitchen with anticipation and found Janie standing on a chair beside Lucy as they dropped rolls of some kind of dough into the skillet. Seeing them like that nearly knocked the breath out of him. His Beth had loved to cook and he visualized her standing there with Janie.

"Pa! I'm frying cornbread." His child beamed at

him and his heart clutched.

Lucy turned uncertainly toward him and their gazes locked. A jolt of awareness socked him in the gut. He was glad to see that she looked as though she felt better. The redness of her skin was nearly gone but he knew that after her long day she had to be tired. Still, she was smiling.

"She's going to be a great cook. She's certainly enthusiastic about learning."

"And apparently from the scents in here you're a good one to teach her."

"Thank you." She shot a wink at Janie. "I had a wonderful helper. She showed me where the storeroom was and we scrounged up everything we needed for vegetable stew and my favorite, fried cornbread."

Trey nodded, his mouth watering more. "I'm fine with it. Really fine. I can't tell you what a pleasant surprise it was to open the door to the scents filling my home." *Or her pretty, smiling face and his child's happy laughter.* The thought hit him hard but there was no denying it was true or the longing for the way things could have been, if Beth had lived.

“Me and Lucy cleaned my room, Pa. You need to come see it. It smells good. It was so fun. And Lucy says I’m a good helper, Pa.”

Trey’s gaze met Lucy’s and he felt very beholden to her for making his child so happy. Lucy had been here for one day and suddenly he felt as if his whole world was shifting.

CHAPTER FOUR

After supper, he went and gathered up his things so Lucy could sleep in his room. Trey didn't have any extra sheets and he couldn't ask her to sleep in his bed, in his sheets…that just was highly improper. His gaze went to the chest at the end of his bed. *Beth's chest.*

Moving forward, he opened it. He knew what was in the chest. He kept everything in it for Janie. He knew there were blankets inside the chest. They might be a little musty but they would be unslept in. The chest was full of keepsakes for Janie. Things that had belonged to her mother that he wanted her to one day have in her own home. Things that Beth would have wanted her to have. He lifted out a set of baby bibs that Beth made for Janie. Pain that had once been overwhelming washed through him, but it wasn't as overwhelming now after six years. Still, he loved Beth—always would. A giant hole in his heart still ached for her.

He thanked God for sparing his baby girl. When he thought about nearly losing both of them, he wasn't able to bear it. Every day that he looked at his beautiful, sweet child who had helped him have something to live for, he was thankful she'd helped him move on with his life.

He carried the blankets to the bed and changed them for the covers that were there. Then he carried his things to the storeroom. Tomorrow they'd work through all of this. But right now he needed to go make his rounds and think.

Lucy was reading a book to Janie when he came into the room.

"I've prepared the room for you. You'll probably

be asleep when I get home from making my rounds. I'll wish you a good night and thank you for watching out for Janie."

"I'm happy to watch out for her. She's a delightful girl." She smiled at Janie, who beamed. "I'll see you in the morning then."

He leaned down and gave Janie a kiss on the top of her head. "I'm hoping you're asleep when I get home too. Now that we have Lucy, we might get you on a little bit better schedule."

"I'm glad Lucy's here now. It'll be better. Lots better."

Trey had a lot on his mind as he settled his hat back on his head then left the room. He paused out on the porch as the picture of Lucy reading to his baby girl lingered in his mind…it had looked so right. So very right…

Her words touched Lucy.

They prepared for bed and she helped the sweet girl put on her nightgown. "Can I brush your hair before you go to sleep?"

"Yes, please. It gets the worst knots in it when I sleep. My pa says I sleep like a wild bear is chasing me."

Lucy chuckled. "You must move a lot."

Janie nodded her head. "Sometimes I go to sleep with my head at one end of the bed and wake up with it on the other end."

"Oh, that is a lot. I'm glad you don't fall off the bed."

"I done that."

"Oh no. Hope you didn't bump your head."

Janie giggled. "The covers went with me so I didn't."

She picked up the brush and had Janie sit on the edge of the bed. "I'll braid it so that way it won't tangle, even if you do roll all around." She brushed gently, working her way through the tangles.

Janie chattered the whole time she brushed. "You do that good. Mrs. Mulberry is nice and so is Miss Essie Jane Tate and Mrs. Murphy but they tug too hard."

"Well, if we keep the tangles tamed better through the day and night, it will be a lot easier to brush from here on out. And I'll teach you how to brush it too."

Janie smiled over her shoulder. "I never had it braided before."

"You'll like it. And tomorrow you'll have pretty waves. Now hop into the bed."

Janie scrambled into the bed. Lucy pulled the covers up to her shoulders and then gently brushed her hair off her face. Janie's big blue eyes studied her solemnly. "I'm glad you're here, Lucy."

Lucy's heart ached for the little girl. She knew so much of how she felt at this age not to have a mommy. She let her mind go back to the stories that her mother used to make up for her before she went to bed. "I'm glad I'm here too. Now, relax and let me tell you a story my momma used to tell me when I was your age. Would you like that?"

Janie nodded and Lucy told her a story about a beautiful fairy princess who lived under a lily pad. It didn't take Janie long before her eyes drifted shut and she fell fast asleep.

Lucy yawned and then slowly got up. She was stove up a little after her long journey by stagecoach and she was tired, too. It had been a very long and draining day.

She blew out the lantern. And then walked toward the second room and entered. She stopped inside the door. Her first impression was how bare the room was. Other than the pretty dresser that looked handmade and then the beautiful quilt on the bed, there was nothing. The quilt, however, was a wedding quilt with quilted intertwined rings that signified the two lives being joined in marriage. Lucy swallowed hard as a lump lodged in the middle of her chest.

The idea that she would be sleeping in his bed using something so obviously cherished hit her hard. She couldn't do it. Earlier that day, Big John and another man had delivered her own chest that had her things in it. She gently folded the quilt and laid it on the dresser. Walking over to her travel chest, she unlatched it and lifted the blankets she'd packed. They were simple but colorful, and they were hers.

She dressed the bed and then crawled into the bed.

She blew the lantern out and settled beneath the covers. She stared up at the dark ceiling for a long time and thought she wouldn't go to sleep quickly because she was so nervous. But she was asleep almost immediately. The last thing she thought about was Trey's handsome face and she felt the twist of disappointment that her dream of being a bride had not come true.

CHAPTER FIVE

The next day, she woke and the sun was streaming in her window. She sat straight up in bed and gasped. *Oh no, she was the housekeeper and hadn't gotten up and fixed breakfast!* Scrambling out of bed, she yanked her gown off and hurriedly pulled on a clean dress. She ran her brush through her long hair and then quickly wound it into a bun on the nape of her head. She freshened up as best she could and then rushed out of her room.

She found Janie sitting at the table, munching on a biscuit. Trey was nowhere to be seen.

"Good morning," Janie said brightly.

Anxiety filled her. *She was the housekeeper. What kind of housekeeper slept in while the employer got up and headed off to work?* "Did you sleep well?" she asked, trying to figure out what she should do first. Now that she'd started the day out so wrong.

"Do you want cornbread and jam? Pa left one for you on the stove."

She bit back a groan. He'd had to eat a cold cornbread and there had only been three pieces left the night before. There were so many questions she needed answered. *Would he be coming home for lunch? Did she need to fix him something?*

"So, your pa has gone to work?"

"He went awhile ago. He told me not to disturb you because you had a long trip the last two days and were probably worn out."

She had been but she couldn't lose sight now that she was just hired help. She could be dismissed at any time if she wasn't doing a good job. This meant she had to do better.

"Okay, well, I was but now I'm all rested. And I

need to do some washing. Can you show me where the washtub is?"

"Oh yes. It's out here on the porch."

Lucy followed Janie out onto the porch and she saw the bed roll where Trey had slept. She cringed. She'd caused the poor man to have to sleep on the floor—not even on a cot—and then she hadn't even fixed him a hot meal for breakfast.

"Here's the washtub. Pa don't use it, though. One of the ladies in town does our washing."

"Well, now I'm here and we're going to do it. We need to get started early, though, because we want your covers to dry before nightfall."

"Oh, I like it when my covers are clean. They smell good, like sunshine and soap all mixed together."

Lucy smiled at the charming look on Janie's face. The little girl was a dear. "Then let's get to it so you can have sunshine in your sleep tonight."

They went outside and over to a pump. She set the tub underneath the spigot and then she worked it—up and down, up and down. It been a few days since she had done any type of labor and it strained her arms.

Janie chattered all morning as they worked, washing sheets and covers. It was a long morning but she enjoyed it despite that it was hot and sweaty work. Mid-morning, they had company.

"Mrs. Mulberry, Miss Essie Jane Tate!" Janie exclaimed as two ladies walked around the corner of the house.

Lucy scrambled to stand and wiped her hands on her apron. Mrs. Mulberry was gray-headed and plump, with a beaming smile. The other lady was thin and timid-looking but had a gentle smile that was just as welcoming as her friend's.

They hugged Janie.

"We came to welcome you to Sweet." Mrs. Mulberry introduced them despite Janie having called out their names.

Lucy introduced herself and invited them inside for some tea.

"Oh, no, we aren't going to interrupt you. We just wanted to welcome you to town. We heard yesterday that you're going to be the sheriff's housekeeper and look out for our little Janie and we were thrilled."

"Oh we were," Miss Essie Jane Tate agreed. "It will be good for them to have a younger female to help out. Our sheriff works too much and needs to have help. What he needs is a wife."

Janie went to pick up her doll that she'd dropped when the ladies arrived.

Mrs. Mulberry said quietly, "We had hoped when we saw you get off the stage yesterday that you might be a mail-order bride. That maybe our good sheriff might have finally realized he needed a wife and mother for Janie. But a housekeeper is better than the way it was."

Lucy said nothing but wished it had been the other way.

"And who knows," Essie Jane said softly. "Maybe love will blossom."

She was shocked at the pink-cheeked suggestion of the thinner lady but instantly thought of her handsome boss…and couldn't help the wistful hope that filled her.

They didn't stay long and soon, feeling welcomed and hopeful, she went back to work. She would make the best of things. And maybe Miss Essie Jane Tate was right. Maybe love would blossom.

Trey was heading home for lunch and to check on Lucy when he ran in to Mrs. Mulberry and Miss Essie Jane Tate.

Mrs. Mulberry smiled as if she'd just had her favorite pie. "Well, good morning, Sheriff. We came to meet Lucy. What a delightful young woman. Janie seems thrilled that you've hired a housekeeper and we are too. I must say that we've been praying for you to find a wife and had hoped that Lucy was a mail-order bride come to marry you."

"Yes," Miss Essie Jane added. "We were quite disappointed to find out otherwise. However, at least you had the good sense to hire her on to watch over Janie. It will be a wonderful asset to your lives."

Mrs. Mulberry tilted her head to the side. "Though, I must add, that with as beautiful as Lucy is, one smart cowboy will surely snatch her from your employment soon and whisk her home to start her own family. And then our little Janie will be right back where she was yesterday…"

"True." Miss Essie Jane clucked and looked sad at the thought. "Then whatever will you do? It will be so sad."

Alarm rang through Trey as he realized what they said was true.

Mrs. Mulberry barely paused. "Well, we won't keep you. We're off to the restaurant for lunch. See you later, young man."

Feeling deeply perplexed, Trey continued to his house and heard Janie's chatter coming from the backyard.

He had had a rough night on the hard floor and had tossed and turned all night. His thoughts had been troubled and he couldn't help thinking about Lucy.

He paused at the corner of the house and listened to Janie and Lucy talking about Janie's dolls.

"I can't believe it—you know how to make more dolls?" Janie exclaimed.

"I do. My mama taught me before she died. And I'll teach you. So it's a good thing to know and it's fun. And we can make doll clothes so you can work on your stitches."

"My mama never got a chance to teach me anything," Janie said, softly. "She died when I was born. I sure wish I got to meet her."

"I wish you got to meet her too."

"I'm glad you came. Maybe my mama sent you in her place."

Trey's heart thundered in his chest, hearing his child's wistful words. *She was longing for her mother. For a mother.* Janie saw him then.

"Pa," she exclaimed and raced toward him. He caught her up in his arms and looked at her and held her there.

She was growing up. Which meant it was more imperative that she was going to need a female around. Someone permanent. And she liked Lucy. *What if someone else swept Lucy off her feet and they lost her?* Mrs. Mulberry's words worried him.

CHAPTER SIX

Doris Nixon owned the restaurant; her husband had passed away about two years ago. Lately, she had been bringing lunch to the office on days when she had time and they had been lingering after church to talk. He knew she was showing interest in him but he had no interest in her in a romantic sense. But they were both young and had both suffered the loss of a loved one. He could not show her unkindness though he had no desire to remarry. However, now that he thought about it, she was an upstanding citizen and pretty. But she had her eyes set on running her business. She didn't really seem as though she was very interested in Janie when they ate at the restaurant. And that really bothered him.

Lucy was wringing out another sheet and a blanket. He could see the muscles in her arms work as she had her sleeves rolled up and her forearms were showing. She was working hard. Had been since yesterday, when she'd taken on the job.

The wet quilt she was wringing out was heavy and she used the back of her hand to push damp hair off her face.

He went to help her. "Here, let me do that."

"Oh no, I have it. I do this all the time."

He reached for the wet quilt anyway. His hands brush hers, much like it had the day before when they'd touched. Sparks raced up his arms and straight to his stomach. Her eyes widened and a small gasp escaped her pretty, pink lips as if she had felt that same tingling.

"I'll help you twist one side out with the other side then."

"Yes sir, if that's what you want," she said.

Her words of agreement unsettled him. He realized he didn't like her saying *yes sir* to him but he was her employer. He cleared his throat and held onto the quilt. It was all scrunched up in a twisted mass. She grabbed the other end and they twisted in opposite directions as water squeezed from the quilt.

He contemplated how to fix the dilemma he found himself in. She was his hired help, so this put a wall between them and her saying *yes sir* was right…but wrong. At last, he just said what was on his mind. "There's no need for you to say yes sir to me."

She wiped her hands on her apron and then pushed another damp strand of hair out of her eyes. Her blonde hair sparkled in the sunlight. "Well, you're my boss. It would be awkward for me not to say it."

He frowned as he took the quilt and hung it on the clothesline. She helped as Janie chased a butterfly. "I strung this when Janie was a baby and I was having to wash her baby things. Just about wore me out there was so much wash." He smiled and Lucy chuckled easily. He liked it very much. He liked *her* very much.

"But you made it. I'm so sorry you had to go

through such a loss. For your sake and hers."

"Thank you." They stared at each other and then she turned and went back to wash something else. "Wait. I came home for lunch and I was thinking since you're new in town that maybe you would enjoy a nice lunch at the restaurant?"

She ran her damp hands down the front of her apron. Her cheeks were pink from the hot water and exertion. Her eyes twinkled in the sun and he wondered whether they'd darken after she was kissed. The thought ambushed him.

"Well, what do you think?" he asked, his mouth dry.

"I'm a sight. I don't think that would be a good idea. There will probably be a lot of people there and I've been washing."

"You look lovely. But if you need to have a few moments to go change, then I'm fine with that too."

"Are we going to lunch?" Janie asked, having overheard them and running up. "Let's go, Lucy. The restaurant has the best pie you ever tasted."

Lucy looked from him to Janie. The joy in Janie's

face must have changed her mind.

"Okay, give me just a moment to tidy my hair and take off my apron." She rolled her sleeves down. "I'll be ready in a moment." She hurried to the house and disappeared inside.

Jamie jumped up and down and Trey felt the warmth of pleasure course through him at the idea that she was going to go have lunch with him. He couldn't think of how long it had been since he shared a meal in public with a woman. He'd shared a meal with her last night but this seemed different.

True to her word, Lucy was gone only a few minutes. She had combed her hair into a neat twist at the back of her neck and he suddenly wondered what it would look like down. He pushed the thought away and admired the soft green dress she'd put on. It wasn't new but it was pretty and was a soft contrast to her eyes. As she stepped off the porch and walked toward him, her hips swayed and he felt a stirring within him. He wanted to offer her his arm but if he escorted her down the street arm-in-arm, everybody in town would be talking more than they already were. Instead, he took Janie's hand.

"I'm takin' two pretty ladies to lunch today. I will have every man in town jealous." Janie giggled and he enjoyed watching her skip along beside him, holding his hand.

As they reached the sidewalk, it seemed as if every man in town tried to make sure they passed them to say good morning to her and tip their hats at her.

By the time they reached the restaurant, he had growled at a few and wasn't so sure this had been a good idea. Mrs. Mulberry's words taunted him.

Lucy would not last long in town before the men would start trying to court her.

At the thought, Trey lost his appetite.

Lucy was feeling awkward as they walked down the sidewalk and men kept saying hello to her. It was a really friendly town but every time a man tipped his hat or said hello, Trey tensed and acted like a grizzly. Surely not; he had definitely said he didn't want to marry her. So she was probably imagining his reactions. She studied each man from beneath her lowered lashes, trying to imagine if one of them came courting. After all, she had come here to get married and just because Trey had decided he didn't want to marry her didn't mean she was off the market. Like Big John had said, she would get to choose her husband this way.

Still, walking beside Trey, so tall, strong, and handsome…there was just no comparison. She knew, especially after being around him over the last twenty-four hours, that she would have a hard time courting anyone else. There was so much about him that she found attractive. His voice—she loved his voice. And she enjoyed watching the way he treated little Janie. That endeared him to her immediately. Even in the letters to her that he hadn't written.

She admired everything about him. She tried to squelch her thoughts. Tried hard as she could to imagine being married to one of the cowboys or farmers who said hello. But she couldn't, considering not one of them felt right. Trey *did* feel right, despite the fact that Trey didn't want anything from her other than her housekeeping and child care services. Her spirits darkened as they crossed the street and headed toward the restaurant.

Flower boxes on the windowsills were bright and welcoming. She tried to talk herself into a better mood. Coming out West to marry a man she never met had been risky. But she had wanted to start a life out here in the West in this raw land that she'd read about back home.

But she wanted some security and a family, and being Trey's housekeeper offered her neither of those dreams. Deep in thought, she stumbled as she walked through the door Trey was holding open for her. He grabbed her arm to keep her from falling.

"Are you okay?"

The heat of his hand on her arm had her heart pounding. The undeniable attraction she felt for him caused her to blush. She had to get a hold of this reaction she felt every time he touched her. She had to quit thinking of him as the man she'd hoped to marry.

She pulled away. "I'm fine. I wasn't paying attention. I was admiring the flowers and the restaurant." It was partly true.

Janie entered the restaurant and looked around. "I think it's pretty too," the child said. "I think one day I might grow up and own a restaurant."

Trey looked at Janie. "One day you might do that if that's what you want. With the way Lucy is teaching you, it would have to be a success."

Hearing him encourage his daughter to do whatever she dreamed was one more thing about Trey that spoke to Lucy's heart.

A woman with beautiful red hair and a heart-shaped face with big green eyes came toward them. She looked as if she had stepped off the society pages back in St. Louis and seemed out of place here in this small-town restaurant. Lucy was busy admiring her as she swept toward them and Lucy couldn't miss that the beautiful lady's sparkling eyes were fixed on Trey.

"Trey, it is so good to see you," she said, in a lilting tone. "I was thinking I was going to have to bring you lunch again at the sheriff's office in order to see you. You are working too many hours."

Lucy saw Trey's color turn a tinge of red. He

looked uncomfortable as his gaze met hers and then darted to Janie. She fought jumping to conclusions but there seemed to be something between him and the beautiful restaurant owner.

"Yes, I've been busy, Doris. I'd like you to meet my, our, new housekeeper. Lucy Calvert. She arrived yesterday on the stage."

Lucy felt relegated to a lower level as Doris inclined her head toward Lucy. Her eyes narrowed as they took in everything about Lucy.

"We've been having lots of fun since she got here," Janie said, taking Lucy's hand.

Doris's gaze flickered to Janie and then back to Trey.

Was it Lucy's imagination or had she just ignored Janie? "We have had fun." Lucy squeezed Janie's hand.

"I heard about her arriving yesterday. About the spectacle you made traipsing down the street to the boardinghouse. I heard she had red splotches all over her."

Lucy didn't like being talked about when she was

standing right there.

"Lucy is allergic to cats and there are several cats at the boardinghouse, so she couldn't stay there."

Doris's expression faltered. "So, if she isn't staying there, where is she staying?"

"At our house," Janie offered, grinning proudly.

"What?"

"Yes, she's staying with us." Trey said. "It's better that way since she's our housekeeper and is looking after Janie. It will work out better that way."

Shock registered on Doris's face. Lucy had assumed everyone in town had heard the news that she was his housekeeper and living in his home.

"She's living in your house?" Doris gasped. "But Trey, this is very inappropriate. You have your young daughter to consider. And you have, well, you have a young female living under your roof with you. That's, it's just not right."

"I have my own room," he offered, a scowl darkening his face. "She has her own room and Janie is in the house. I don't see any other way to do it."

"I would think you would get her her own place.

Or, better yet hire an older woman. Not a…a…" Her gaze raked down Lucy. "A woman, it seems, who welcomes gossip."

Stunned, Lucy cringed. Her first impression of the beautiful woman had been so wrong. Mortified she couldn't form any words as she stood there in the middle of the restaurant wondering what everyone else in town was thinking about her.

CHAPTER SEVEN

Trey tried to hide his anger. Seething down deep, he grated his teeth. He saw the flicker of pain and humiliation in Lucy's eyes. And it bothered him something fierce. Lucy had been nothing but kind to them since she had arrived here in a very awkward and hard situation. And she handled herself with grace and kindness always. He had thought he'd taken control of their awkward situation by hiring her as his housekeeper when she'd arrived as his mail-order bride. But now, Doris's attitude bothered him. How many other people were thinking the same thing?

His gaze flickered around the dining area. Mrs. Mulberry and Miss Essie Jane Tate waved and smiled. *What did they think? If they had set him and Lucy up, had they anticipated that he would not go through with their plan?*

Mrs. Mulberry scurried from her table and rushed to them. He was relieved and wondered whether the older woman had sensed something was wrong.

"You three must join us. Doris, would you get another chair for our table?" Her eyes were bright and welcoming.

Relief washed over Trey and he thought hopefully it wasn't going to be as bad as he began to think.

"Did you know she spent the night at Trey's house last night?" Doris asked Mrs. Mulberry.

The older lady frowned. "Yes, but I'm sure it was quite respectable. Janie was there and Lucy is a lovely lady and our sheriff is a very honorable man."

"But…you know this isn't respectable." Doris gasped.

Trey glanced at Lucy and saw her skin pale as she looked down.

"I've been thinking, and should have offered a room at my home immediately," Mrs. Mulberry said, still ignoring Doris. "I can assure you that I have no cats. I think they are adorable little creatures but I, too, am allergic. Break out in the most awful red hives. My Mr. Mulberry, rest his sweet soul, gave me a kitten as a wedding gift and very nearly killed me right there. So I do understand. However, seeing as you are there to watch out for Janie, you may want to continue being a live-in housekeeper."

Trey suddenly realized that he had made a terrible mistake.

"I'm not sure," Lucy began. "I think, given the circumstances, that that might be a very kind offer." Her cheeks were pink and he saw the humiliation there.

He had caused her to feel that way.

Doris had unknowingly brought him to his senses.

Lucy had been exhausted yesterday and yet she had worked and played with his daughter and then fell asleep in his room, compromising her reputation. She came here thinking she was getting married and now had people like Doris saying unfair and humiliating things about her. How could he have been such a fool?

"Mrs. Mulberry. That is a very kind offer and I think under the circumstances that would be very agreeable.. But right now, at this moment, could Janie sit with you for a few minutes and then we will join you soon?"

"Certainly."

"Thank you." He took Lucy's elbow and moved her outside. He had things to fix.

Lucy stared at him with alarm in her eyes. He held his temper. This was his fault, not hers. Feeling protective of Lucy, he tried hard not to look angry as he took her elbow and escorted her out onto the steps of the restaurant.

She walked beside him with quiet dignity as they walked down the sidewalk. It ended and he continued on toward the small church. He didn't really know where he was taking them but when he saw the church yard, he knew. There was a bench beneath a big cottonwood tree.

An internal conflict battled inside him. There were so much to consider, so many things that he had done wrong. Even though he did not ask for any of this, it was his to fix.

Lucy still said nothing as he opened the gate and led her to the bench under the shade tree.

"Would you sit?" he asked.

She sank to the edge of the bench, her back stiff and her cheeks still pink. He couldn't even imagine what she must be thinking.

"We need to talk." He sat on the bench beside her. It was small and they were very close; their shoulders touched.

"I must apologize. I've put you in a very compromising situation. I didn't mean to do that. I thought I was helping yesterday."

"We were both startled yesterday." She kept her gaze down.

He reached for her hand. "You came a long way and I don't really know all that much about you but I can tell you're a good and decent and kind person. You have been very accommodating and kindhearted to my Janie and I'm sorry that you had those harsh things said back there by Doris. In a way, though, I'm glad. She opened my eyes to what I was doing. I can't tell you how badly I feel." He paused and then cleared his throat. "My Beth, she was a very good person. And after she gave birth to Janie, she didn't last long and drifted away from us. Since then, I threw myself into my work and I tried to do right by Janie."

Her lashes lifted and she looked at him. "You are a wonderful father."

Her words hit him hard. "Thank you. But obviously, someone in town realized my child needed a mother. I thought we were doing fine but since you arrived yesterday, I have realized how much my daughter misses having her mother. I don't have a clue who brought you here. I thought it might be Mrs. Mulberry and her church quilting club but now I'm not so sure. But that's not important right now. When it comes to remarrying, I've been thinking only of myself. Someone realized that I've done an injustice to my Janie by not even considering looking for a mother for her." His chest tightened as he realized what he was about to say. Lucy's brows had dipped.

"Janie means the world to me. I really want her to be happy. She needs a mother. In the short time that you have been in her life, you've already made a difference. I've never seen her get on with anybody like she gets on with you. So, I guess what I'm saying is that the housekeeper situation isn't going to work."

Lucy's gaze riveted to him and she paled. "Okay, I guess I can look for work somewhere else then. Maybe Mrs. Mulberry will let me stay with her—" Her hand trembled in his.

He smiled and squeeze gently. "No, that's not what I meant. I meant that I think we should take Mrs. Mulberry up on her offer, if that's what you think. I don't want to compromise your reputation any more. But, I'd like to ask if you would consider honoring your original intent when you came to town. Would you…" He stumbled over his words. Sweat beaded on his forehead and his stomach churned. "What I'm saying is I think we should go ahead with the marriage."

Her eyes widened to the size of wagon wheels. "You want to marry me?"

"Yes." He wasn't sure whether he was doing right or wrong, but he knew she was a good woman and would take care of and love his daughter. And if something were to happen to him, he could rest easy that she was the kind of woman who would continue to take care of Janie.

"But what about Doris? I can tell that you and she—"

"Have no future. I want a mother for Janie who will love her and care for her. And that's you. But it's up to you. If you don't want that, then we'll talk to Mrs. Mulberry and see if you can stay with her and just come to the house in the daytime."

"No, I want to honor my original commitment. I want to marry you."

He swallowed as her words sank in. He took a deep breath. "Good. We can work the details out over the next two days. I think you being a housekeeper isn't going to work for you. Coming into the household as my wife and Janie's mother would be quite satisfactory. I'm not sure how these things work, honestly, and I'm totally in the dark and baffled. I know I'm a stranger to you but you came all this way just knowing my name."

She chuckled. "I had your two letters and they were long. And I've learned since being here that whoever wrote those letters knows you very well. I have come to the decision that they did it from a good heart because everything they conveyed through their words about you is true. You are honest, love your daughter and…so much more."

He was thankful that whoever had sent the letters had high opinions of him. "So, you're sure, now that you've met me, you're sure you still willing to marry me? It can be, at least until you ready to change it, in name only. I am just trying to do right by my daughter."

He thought he saw a flicker of disappointment… He wasn't sure what he saw. And suddenly he realized that they had a ways to go but he wanted her to think highly enough of him that she was sure. About everything.

He didn't know what circumstances had driven her from St. Louis to become a mail-order bride but something had pushed her to take on the uncertain, and probably scary, endeavor for a woman alone. He hoped she would open up and tell him about her past soon. But right now he waited—anticipated—her answer.

Lucy's heart fluttered and then pounded like a locomotive in her chest. Her stomach churned and she was so aware of the warm feel of his hand as he gently clasped hers between them. *He had asked her to marry him.* For a moment, the dream of finding a man to love her slammed hard against her heart walls. He was giving her a second chance to decide to say no but she was fortunate and grateful…to be blessed that she had come all this way and found such a good man to marry.

She looked into his beautiful warm eyes and nodded. "Yes, I still want to marry you. It would give me a sense of stability and would save my reputation. Yesterday, when I arrived, it was a shocking and unanticipated event. I'll be a good wife to you. And be a loving mother to Janie. My own mother died when I was young. I had a few years with her and much of that time was with her being bedridden. After she died, I lived with my aunt but she was a housekeeper of a wealthy family and didn't have much time to spend with me. I could have married in St. Louis but I wanted out of the city. I wanted to come West." Her excitement in her words was stronger now and she readjusted to the idea that she was going to be his wife. The idea thrilled her. "On the trip here, I loved it. It was hard but this land is beautiful and being on the frontier is exciting to me. Building a life here is what I want and your letter, or the letter I thought was from you, touched me and gave me the strength to take the step and reach for my dream. I can't thank you enough for that."

Something odd and uncertain shone in his eyes. And suddenly she wondered whether she had said too much. His gaze hovered on her lips.

"I'm not sure I'm comfortable with you thanking me," he said. "I should be thanking you because I feel in my heart that you will be a wonderful mother for Janie and for that I'm forever grateful to you. As a lawman, my job has dangers and I worry about her when I have to lead a posse. It gives me peace knowing she'll be with you the next time I have to ride out."

She hadn't thought about the dangers. Fear seized her. *What if something happened to him?*

"I think we should marry within the next couple of days. Do you agree?"

This was what she had been waiting for. She said a quick prayer. God had brought her this far and she was going to trust him now. "Two days is fine."

He stood and tugged her to a standing position and to her complete and utter surprise, he pulled her into his arms and hugged her close. "Thank you," he whispered against her temple. Her knees were weak as his arms tightened around her.

"So, let's go tell Janie. She's going to be thrilled."

They walked back to the restaurant and this time he had her hand resting in the crook of his arm with his hand resting over it. She was still trying to adjust to what had just transpired when they reentered the restaurant. *She was going to be his bride.*

She was astounded and thrilled at the idea. She had come here on the stage with some trepidation but now, knowing him, she was filled with excitement and anticipation.

The moment they reentered the restaurant, Doris glided, like a princess, toward them. A beautiful smile was plastered on her flawless face. Lucy almost felt sorry for her.

"Trey, I hope I didn't say anything to upset you a few minutes ago. I only said what I thought needed to be said."

Trey smiled and patted Lucy's hand. "Lucy has agreed to be my wife. I'm a very happy man." He smiled at Lucy. "We will be married on Saturday morning. Now, we need to go tell Janie."

Doris gasped and took a step back. "But, this wasn't what I had… Trey, this is so sudden."

Trey shook his head. "Not really. Now if you'll excuse us, we're going to go celebrate with Janie and Mrs. Mulberry and Miss Essie Jane Tate."

They moved to the table. He held the chair for Lucy as she sat down beside Janie and then he sat beside her and smiled all around at everyone. "We have news."

The ladies were smiling as if they knew something good was coming. Lucy was nervous now.

"Janie," he said. "I've asked Lucy to marry me. How do you feel about that?"

She gasped. "You're going to be my mother?"

The older ladies had instantly burst into grins but Lucy held her breath as she nodded at the dear child. "Is that okay with you? I'll be your second mother since your first mother can't be here."

Tears filled Janie's eyes and she threw her arms around Lucy.

CHAPTER EIGHT

Mrs. Mulberry was thrilled to have Lucy at her home. She had a lovely home and Lucy found the little woman endearing. She gave her a hug as she got out of the wagon.

"Oh my goodness, I am so excited that you are here."

Trey said he'd be back for her in the morning and Janie hugged her tightly, which did Lucy's heart good. As soon as they were gone, Mrs. Mulberry clasped her hands together and sighed heavily.

"So sweet. I knew this was going to be a match

made in heaven the moment I saw you get off that stage. Come into the house, dear. We'll have some warm tea and cookies."

Had Mrs. Mulberry been the one who wrote those letters? Lucy really didn't think so, but yet her words pointed that way. After all, Trey hadn't been there to meet the stage. Still, Lucy had the feeling the letters had been written by a man. Then again, men weren't known to write great letters, so she could be wrong. *Maybe Mrs. Mulberry meant she knew it after she saw her and Trey together?*

"Do you have a special dress for the occasion with you?"

"I have a new one that I made."

"Wonderful. Bring it tomorrow when you come back and I'll make sure it's fluffed and wrinkle-free for the wedding on Saturday morning. Essie Jane is going to come on Saturday and do your hair up for you. She's very good at doing. You'll be a vision when she is finished with you. The sheriff will be knocked over when he sees you marching up the aisle toward him."

Lucy had a feeling that her wedding was

completely out of her hands now. She nodded and thought about her future. It was going to be wonderful. She felt so blessed.

And there was a hope in her heart that one day maybe Trey could love her. When he'd spoken of his first wife, Lucy had longed to know love like she saw in his eyes and heard in his gentle words. And she prayed that with time, maybe he could come to love her at least a little like he'd loved Beth.

The next morning, Trey picked Lucy up and brought her back to his house. He'd thought about her all night long. Janie had too. She was so excited and that overcame any worries that he had about what he was about to do.

It was a practical marriage. Not one of love. But he was drawn to Lucy and he knew it. He hadn't considered marrying again, determined after having loved once and lost that he wouldn't go through that again. So this marriage of practicality was the best thing for him. It made sense.

He felt guilty knowing he was taking that possibility away from Lucy but she seemed fine with it and that was what mattered.

The following morning, he drove to Mrs. Mulberry's to pick up Lucy. Anticipation hummed through him. "Did you have a good evening?" he asked as he escorted her to the wagon. He could feel Mrs. Mulberry's gaze on them from behind the curtain in the house. He held out his hand and helped her climb up into the wagon.

"I did. We had a wonderful time. Mrs. Mulberry is a lovely lady." She leaned close and whispered, "She talks a lot but still, she is so nice."

He laughed, finding her completely charming. "Yes, she does but she has been wonderful to Janie, and I'm with you on thinking she is a very nice lady." As he drove down the street, he said what he'd been thinking. "I'm wondering if she might have sent those letters?"

"I actually have been wondering that too. I've heard that sometimes in these situations the women's church groups are responsible. But I keep thinking the letters sounded like a man wrote them. Do you have any idea if there is a man in town who might have done it?"

"A man? I can't think of any man who would do that."

She was quiet for a few minutes as they both thought.

"Are you having second thoughts?"

Her question startled him. "No. Are you?" Fear filled him at the thought she was going to back out of their commitment. *What would he tell Janie?*

"No, I'm not. I was just making sure you hadn't had second thoughts."

"Janie's heart would be broken if we backed out now."

"We won't let that happen." She smiled and his heart tugged at the sparkle in her eyes. "I promise."

On Friday night after she fixed supper for Trey and Janie, he had actually taken her arm and promised her everything would work out. Then he brought her back to Mrs. Mulberry's. He hopped from the wagon and came to help her down. He placed his hands around her waist and lifted her to the ground and Lucy felt the warmth of his hands all the way through her. Instead of letting her go and walking with her to the front door, he took her hand.

"Do you need anything? I let Mr. Sweet at the mercantile know you would be on my account. So, if you need anything, get it. Or if you need me to get it and bring it to you before the wedding, let me know."

"Thank you," she said, breathless as her heart raced. "I think I'm fine, though." She tried not to stare at him but she was mesmerized by the man who would soon be her husband.

He nodded and then walked her up the path to the front door of Mrs. Mulberry's. Under one arm, he carried the box she'd brought that contained her dress and with the other, he continued to hold her hand. Her heartbeat thundered and she reminded herself that this was in name only and that he was marrying her because he needed a mother for his sweet daughter. Not because he was looking for a wife for himself. Not because he had sent for her. No, this was a name-only marriage and the fact that he was holding her hand was simply because Trey was a genuinely nice man.

And she was grateful for that.

Her heartbeat raced as she looked up into his earnest eyes and wished for more. She longed suddenly for his love…wishing this wedding was truly for love and not just for practical reasons. When he dipped his head and kissed her, she could hardly breathe. It was a tender kiss, gentle and brief, and when he stepped back, it left her wishing for more with every fiber of her being.

He stepped back, his brows cinched together, and then he replaced his hat, his gaze wavering. "I'll see you tomorrow at the church. Sleep good. Tomorrow will be a long day."

And then he turned and strode from the porch and climbed into the wagon. He had no idea the turmoil his kiss had kicked up inside her. The longing that filled her was something she'd never experienced.

She touched her lips with her fingertips as butterflies roamed through her. Tomorrow she would be his bride and her new life would officially begin.

The door opened behind her and she jumped.

"That was one sweet kiss. I was coming to open the door for you when I saw the two of you kissing through the glass. Oh, the memories of my Calvin came rushing back in those moments." She waved a hand in front of her face as if she were hot and indeed her cheeks were rosy. "Well, anyway, young love is a wonderful thing."

"But he doesn't love me—"

Mrs. Mulberry's gaze snapped to her. "He shall. I have no worry about that. Everyone around can see the way he looks at you. He has things to work through but love will grow."

Lucy followed the older woman inside, praying that what Mrs. Mulberry said was true.

Mrs. Mulberry led her back into the parlor, where tea and scones were set out. Clearly she intended to talk some more this evening.

"This is just so exciting. We're celebrating with my sweet cherry scones and tea."

Lucy didn't have the heart to tell the excited Mrs.

Mulberry that she had misinterpreted Trey's hand-holding. Instead, she settled into the soft cushioned chair as Mrs. Mulberry chattered away about the wedding. She made wonderful scones and said that she and several of the church ladies had fixed up desserts for a reception after the wedding. "I just love baking. I love to eat the treats too much, though, and my hips show it. But a little cushion never hurt anyone." She chuckled as she sipped her tea and took another bite of the cherry scone.

Lucy ate two and would have eaten a third one but did not want to appear completely rude. She would probably be too nervous after the wedding tomorrow to even think about eating anything. The idea that there was going to be a reception touched her. The ladies had thought of everything.

When they were finished, they went to the bedroom, where Mrs. Mulberry took the dress out of the box and shook it out and then draped it over the bed.

"It is just lovely," she gasped, looking at the pale-blue dress with tiny flowers embroidered at the neckline and around the waistline. "Did you do this beautiful needlework?"

"I did. My mother taught me at a young age before she passed away. I would sit on her bed with her and she would show me the stitches."

Mrs. Mulberry's eyes misted. "Your mother was very talented and obviously passed it down to you. Little Janie is going to enjoy you teaching this to her."

"Thank you. My mother would have wanted it that way."

And it was true. Though she knew her mother would have wanted her to marry for love, she felt as though she would approve the course Lucy had taken. Helping a motherless child was the next best thing to having one of her own.

"Pa, I'm really getting Lucy as my mama this morning?" Janie had come busting into his room before the rooster crowed.

Trey had rubbed the sleep out of his eyes as he sat up in bed. He hadn't slept until the wee hours of the morning and then only because exhaustion had set in. Now he felt as if a stagecoach had rolled over him and then drug him across a rock-strewn prairie. His daughter, on the other hand, looked bright-eyed as a baby rabbit. “Yes, you are.” His voice cracked with dryness. “Let me get up and I’ll fix us some breakfast.”

“Oh, Pa, I just can’t believe it. I’ve been praying for so long that she would come and now that she’s here it just seems too good to be true. She’s not going to leave, is she?”

He cocked his head to the side and studied her. He pulled her small body into his chest and hugged her. “No,” he said against her hair. “She isn’t.” *At least, God willing*, he said to himself. He might not let himself fall in love again but he was opening his daughter up for hurt again. He didn’t know any other way to heal the hole in her little heart.

“Good. Then this is going to be the best day of my life.”

He chuckled. “Then I guess we better get up and start getting ready for it.”

“That would be good. We’ve already dusted and

cleaned."

He looked around the storeroom he was using for a bedroom and realized that he and Lucy would have to get the sleeping situation figured out. This might be for practical reasons but he had a nice, soft, big bed in his room that he hoped she would let him share. If they ever decided to take the marriage vows to another level, that would be up to her. If he was marrying her, then it would be his responsibility to give her a child if she wanted it. She was young and there was no reason that he could deny her that. But he would leave that to her.

The thought of that next step affected him in a swift and intense way and he pushed the idea out of his mind. Best to focus on his daughter right now. After all, that was why he was doing this.

That was the only reason he was doing this.

CHAPTER NINE

The wedding chapel was a white clapboard with four steps to a small porch. Someone had hung a few bundles of wild flowers tied with bows on the end of the railing but it was Trey and Janie on the steps that had her attention. He wore his dark pants and it was one of the first things Lucy noticed as Samuel drove her and Mrs. Mulberry and Essie Jane to the chapel.

"I hope you like the soft touches the girls did for the ceremony." Essie Jane's deep gray hair, combed into a tight bun, in no way hinted at her talent with hair. Lucy felt self-conscious with her hair swept to the side and curls hanging against her neck while part of it was swept into a double bun. She had never had anything like this done to her hair and felt quite like a high society lady.

As soon as they came to a halt everyone scrambled from the wagon. "You stay there," Mrs. Mulberry declared and let that handsome future husband of yours help you down."

Lucy couldn't move anyway as she watched Trey stride down the path with sweet Janie trailing after him. He looking so handsome that he stole her breath right out of her chest. He smiled at her and heat suffused her and her heart thundered as she remembered their kiss. He had his hat off and it looked as though he had gotten a haircut. She had the momentary thought that it was a sad thing because she'd liked the curl of his hair at the nape of his neck. He smiled up at her and Janie was jumping at his side, all grins.

"Good morning. You look beautiful."

Her cheeks burned hot at his compliment and she tried to focus on what to say. "Thank you," was all she could come up with as she slipped her hand into his and felt the warmth of him all the way to her toes.

“I’m so excited I could bust,” Janie exclaimed, hopping from one foot to the other. “And Pa is right. You do look beautiful. I love your hair.”

She had momentarily forgotten about her hair. And feeling breathless, she wondered whether Trey liked it. Not that she would be able to wear it like this very often considering she didn’t think Miss Essie Jane would come over every morning and do it for her.

“I’m glad you like it. Miss Essie Jane did it. She is very talented, isn’t she?”

“Very. I would love to have mine like that.”

“Oh honey,” the older lady said, “I can sure do it one day. I’ll come over and we’ll have a play day. As a matter of fact, maybe tonight you can come over to my house or Ambrosia’s house and I’ll do it for you. That would be a perfect plan for this evening. Don’t you think Sheriff?”

Janie’s brow furrowed. “Who is Ambrosia?”

Essie Jane chuckled. “Mrs. Mulberry, dear. Sorry to confuse you.”

"I like that," Janie said and repeated *Ambrosia*. "Can I go, Pa?"

"We'll see," Trey murmured, never taking his eyes off Lucy as the conversation took place behind him.

Lucy's mouth had gone dry and when heHe reached up and lifted her from the wagon and slowly set her on her feet in front of him. Her heart thundered and her knees felt weak. Then he smiled and crooked his elbow.

"Right now we are going to have a wedding. Are you ready for that, Janie?"

"Oh yes, I am.." Janie spun and skipped toward the church and the older ladies hustled up the path behind her.

"Shall we?" he asked Lucy.

"Yes," she said softly and slipped her hand into the crook of his arm as butterflies fluttered through her.

The pastor Jarred Andrews was around Trey's age and very handsome. Lucy hadn't expected a preacher out here in the West to be young. But then she really didn't know all that much about preachers or the West.

He took her hand. "It's nice to meet you, Lucy. We're glad to have you in our town. We think highly of your future husband and Janie. They need you."

She knew his words were true but she also knew that she needed them too…

A few minutes later, they stood at the front of the chapel and to her surprise, people were inside waiting. Big John was sitting off to the side, as was Chester Sweet; a few other shop owners were scattered around the sanctuary.

And more rushed in as they took their places before the preacher.

Preacher Andrews pronounced them husband and wife, and everyone stood and clapped.

"This is just wonderful," Mrs. Mulberry said, calling everyone's attention. "We'll be having cake and scones in the parlor."

"Scones! I tell you what it is a great day," Chester said to Big John. "We'll need to be having more of these weddings if it gets the womenfolk to bake up the goodies. I have the mercantile but since my Lois went to be with the Lord, I miss scones."

Big John grinned. "Well, Chester, I've been telling you that your Lois has been gone now for five years. She wouldn't begrudge you marrying again. You could live to be older than dirt and that's a very long time to live without a mate."

Chester glared at him. "I said I missed scones. It's no call to marry again. And even if I did, who would I marry? Besides that, you're single. Maybe *you* should marry."

Big John had no need to marry again. "I cook my own scones if I want them."

"Well, share with me sometime. Or help figure out a way to get some more of these mail-order brides to town so the women will bake more."

Mrs. Mulberry passed by and overheard Chester. "Maybe you should come to a few church functions and then you'd get a few more scones."

Chester frowned. "Have you ever thought about selling some of your scones to my store?"

Big John almost laughed out loud at the look Mrs. Mulberry gave Chester. "No, I haven't thought about it. But if you think there could be a market for them, I might consider it. Or are you doing this just to get me to bake you scones?"

Chester rubbed his jaw and squinted at her. "Well, now that you mention it, I think that might be a way to help us both."

Big John watched the two frown at each other. Finally Mrs. Mulberry hoisted her chin up and looked down her nose at Chester. "I'll think about it. But right now we better get in there and celebrate this wedding. I am so happy for Trey, Janie, and Lucy. I don't know who sent for her but I like it."

Big John followed her into the little room off the side of the church. Essie Jane was already handing out punch and desserts. Chester almost broke out in a run to get in line. Big John couldn't help feeling a sense of pride as he watched Trey and Janie sipping punch and eating scones. Lucy wasn't eating but he figured the poor girl had to be nervous though she didn't look it, she looked happy.

He moved to stand beside her. "Congratulations on your marriage. You looked like a scared little girl the day you stepped off that stagecoach a few days ago. But today you look like you're not scared at all."

"I'm not scared. But I am nervous. When I came on the stagecoach, I was a little scared because of the uncertainty of not knowing what was waiting for me. And then upon meeting Trey and him not having sent for me, well, that was unnerving. But, now that I've met him and he is such a good man…well, to be quite honest, I know I have nothing to be scared about. I've been very lucky things have turned out good for me. And then there is Janie. I adore her."

Big John wanted to ask her about love but then, he'd sworn when he jumped into this that he would stay out of everyone's business. If he asked too much or seemed too interested, someone might suspect it was him. If he wanted to keep bringing women to town, then he needed to keep it under wraps. And truth was he had his sights set on Preacher Jarred. He'd just replied to a nice letter he'd read of a little lady who he thought might be a match… He'd been watching the preacher take care of everyone in town, sometimes working round the clock seeing sick folks and new babies and helping out in the fields when someone was too sick to tend to their fields. He was a really good man who would give anyone the shirt off his back if he needed to. And the way Big John saw it, the man needed a home and hearth and sweetness of a bride for himself.

But, for now, he studied Trey and caught him studying his new bride with a look of wonder. As if the sheriff couldn't quite believe he was actually married. The next few months would be interesting as these two got themselves situated and used to married life. And each other. And if Big John's prayers were answered, love would enter into the marriage and make it a perfect union.

Only the good Lord had the ability to make that match last.

CHAPTER TEN

About an hour later, Trey leaned close. "I'm sorry to break things up but I'm going to have to go back to work soon and make my rounds."

"Oh, that's perfectly fine," Lucy whispered, almost too quickly. She was feeling the pressure and though everyone was nice, she was ready to go. There were uncertainties to face and things to be done.

When she looked up, Essie Jane and Mrs. Mulberry were smiling widely.

"Okay, everyone," Mrs. Mulberry said, as if taking her cue. "It's time to wish these newlyweds goodnight." Everyone rushed over. Essie Jane grabbed her in a big bear hug with real scrawny arms and looked at her with a serious expression. "You have a wonderful night, my dear. And me and Mrs. Mulberry will take your Janie. Don't you worry about her at all. You and that handsome sheriff have a wonderful wedding night."

Mrs. Mulberry's cheeks were kind of pink. "Yes, Janie will come home with us and you two lovebirds can go back to the house all alone tonight."

Lucy was mortified. Her gaze automatically locked on Trey's and she could feel redness from the top of her head to the tips of her toes. Right now, or maybe forever, this was a wedding in name only. A commitment. But not in that way. And to have everyone in town thinking… Trey looked almost as horrified as she felt. And that didn't sit well with her either. He glanced at Mrs. Mulberry. As others gathered round, he leaned in toward them. "Thank you, ladies, but we will be taking Janie home with us."

The two older ladies both looked as horrified as she felt but for different reasons.

"But, what about marital duties?" Mrs. Mulberry whispered to him.

He nearly choked on the sip of punch he had been taking. "We will take care of ourselves from here on out," he said firmly. He set the cup down. "Thank you, ladies, for all you've done but we have it now." And with that, he took her elbow and escorted her toward the exit, calling Janie from where she had been playing with a friend in the corner by the cake and scones. "Janie, time to go."

Janie raced forward, her hair bobbing. "I can't believe I'm getting to go home with my mama and my pa. I didn't know if I would ever get to say that in one sentence."

Lucy's butterflies were going crazy. "I'm so excited to be your mama. Let's go home. I'm going to read you a bedtime story."

The delight on Janie's face was enough. At least she hoped so. *For now anyway...*

The next few days were busy. Trey had continued to

sleep in the storeroom. She and Janie busied themselves during the day getting the house in order while he was at work. They made pillows from material that they had gone to the mercantile and picked out together. Now the chair had a pillow and a brightly colored tablecloth adorned the table. They had also purchased a beautifully colored small vase that she placed in the center of the table and they put a few wildflowers in.

"Its so beautiful," Janie cooed, clapping her hands together in delight.

"Next year we will plant some flowers and we'll have our own flowers to put on the table."

That statement alone brought another smile to Janie's lips that she had gotten used to seeing. It delighted her.

"I can't wait," Janie gushed.

The busy days passed and Lucy was happy she had a home of her own, with a handsome husband and a delightful child. But in the evenings, after Trey came home, he'd begun to get quieter than he used to be.

They would eat dinner and then he would go on his rounds and she would put Janie to bed. There was no denying that a strain had developed between them.

Though he was polite, he seemed to be becoming more uncomfortable with her than comfortable. She found herself wanting to stare at him or trying more to hide her looks at him below her eyelashes. She didn't want him to catch her staring but she wondered when or if he had plans to ever move into the room with her.

And that thought caused her to feel a little bit lightheaded. They had been married a little over a week when finally one night, after Janie was tucked in, she waited up for him to return from his rounds and found him sitting outside, staring up at the sky. He heard her come outside and turned to look at her. Even in the darkness, she felt his gaze rake over her. She had let her hair down but had waited to change into her nightgown. She wasn't sure what she was going to say to him but she hated the fact that he was sleeping on that cot in the storage room. And Janie had asked her whether mamas and pas shared a room.

She had also asked her when she was going to get a baby sister or brother.

Trey tensed, seeing Lucy with her hair down. His gut tightened and he felt his brow furrow. Since they had gotten married, something had happened and it had become increasingly hard to be around Lucy. The truth was, she was making his house into a home. His daughter smiled all the time and then he was waking up and his pretty little wife fixed him breakfast and smiled brightly.

With each passing day his bed roll was getting lumpier and his mood darker.

Now, she was here in the moonlight, with her big blue eyes shining in the full moon's light and causing every fiber in him to long to hold her.

"It's a pretty night," she said. "Do you mind if I come sit with you?"

His brows dipped. "No. Is everything all right?"

She sank to the bench beside him and gave him a timid smile. "Everything is fine. Just fine…um, how about with you?"

"Fine," he said, his throat suddenly raspy.

Her small breasts rose quickly in the moonlight as she took shallow breaths. He forced his gaze away and tried to think about wanted posters of ugly outlaws-not how beautiful his wife was.

"You sure seem to stay out on your rounds late these days."

"Just making sure the town is secure," he bristled.

"Oh, of course. I was just wondering if that was how it normally was. Or if, well, if you were avoiding coming home?"

Her question stunned him. And hit home. "Why would I do that?"

She glanced at him and he thought he saw moisture gathering in the corners of her eyes. Guilt swamped him and he fought it off. He was purely in survival mode right now.

"I've been worrying about you sleeping on that lumpy cot. I feel guilty taking your bed. It's a big bed. You…well, you could use part of it."

He bit his tongue and fought off yelping. "Um,

I'm not sure that's a good idea."

"Oh," she said.

They sat there in silence and he told himself to say something. But he couldn't because despite the temptations he'd been feeling, he'd also realized that making love to his bride and not loving her wouldn't feel right. And his heart belonged to Beth…

After a moment, Lucy rose. "I think I'll go to bed. Goodnight."

"Lucy," he said and she stopped a few feet away. He struggled with himself. "Sleep good."

She stared at him for a moment and then, without saying anything, went inside.

He felt the world on his shoulders as he watched her go.

Lucy forced herself to go through the next day with a smile on her face for Janie. And she also forced herself to do it the next day too. Trey left both mornings before she was up and he didn't come home until after she was in her room, in her big bed alone.

She was heartsick and hurt and didn't know what to do. She had fallen in love with her husband and now realized he could not love her. His heart belonged to Beth and always would. She only reminded him of what he had lost. She had gone over it in her head night after night and was convinced now that that was what was going on.

And she didn't know how to fix that. *How did she compete with a beloved memory?*

CHAPTER ELEVEN

Trey stomped down the sidewalk two weeks after having married Lucy and everyone who was smart moved out of his way. Samuel had begun to continually avoid him, ducking into the office and then hurrying to make daytime rounds just so he could stay out of Trey's path.

Something had to be done and Trey knew it. Going to sleep thinking about Lucy and waking up thinking about her was driving him mad.

The fact that he did love her didn't make things any better. It made things worse. Since coming outside and inviting him to share the bed with her and his rejection, all he could think about was the look in her eyes. He'd hurt her and he didn't know how to fix it.

A drunk barreled out of the saloon and staggered into the street, and then fell face first into the mud and horse manure. Trey stomped out into the street and yanked the man up by the collar.

"Wha-ya doin'," the drunk muttered.

"I'm keeping you from drowning in horse poop. Or getting run over by wagons out here in the dark, though as drunk as you are you'd never know whether you died or not," Trey growled as he practically dragged the man over to the buckboard full of supplies and hoisted him up onto the floorboard. He could sleep it off. It would serve Milton right, to wake up stinking to high heavens.

Milton didn't even seem to notice as he'd already rolled over and started singing about his one true love. He grinned up at Trey.

Trey shook his head and moved on down the street. Sometimes his job was downright dirty.

He crossed the street to check the doors to the

mercantile and then moved on toward the church. From there, he'd head home. His stomach growled, thinking about the fine meal Lucy had probably cooked tonight. She'd been leaving it on the stove the last two nights and he'd slinked in there and eaten it when he'd finally gone home. He thought about her sleeping in his bed and kissing her sweet lips—thoughts like this were not helping him.

After he checked the church, making sure no drunks were sleeping it off on the steps, he headed around back. The preacher's small house was back there and Trey always passed it on his way home. His boots were dragging as he went. He saw the preacher leaning against the porch post, staring up at the stars.

"Preacher," he said, slowing. He often found Jarred like this, especially the night before services on Sunday morning. "You thinkin' about your sermon for in the morning?"

"Some. Mostly I'm just getting out of the quietness of my house. Some nights the walls seem to cave in around me. How about you—are you hurrying home to your pretty new wife?"

Trey walked over to the picket fence. He hadn't ever thought about whether the preacher might get lonesome and if he wasn't in such an irritable state about his own circumstances, he might have felt bad for the preacher.

"It's not lonesome at my place," he grunted instead, feeling more irritable by the moment. "The truth is, Preacher, I've been dragging my feet on going home because…" He paused, realizing what he'd been about to confess.

"Ah, are you and your wife having some trouble? Need to talk about it?"

"It don't seem right talking about it. But I'm struggling."

"And why would that be?"

"Because I'm sleeping on a hard cot in the storeroom and it's getting mighty old. Especially with having to go to bed in there every night after seeing her…pretty face."

"A cot?" Jarred stopped leaning against the porch post. In the dim light of the lamp coming through the single window on the house, Trey could see the disbelief on the man's face. "Why are you sleeping on a cot?"

"Because that's where I started. I married Lucy so Janie would have a mama, not so I'd have a bed mate. But it's getting harder and harder to go to that storeroom every night."

"Then move into your bedroom. You two are married and that is what married folks do, you know."

"Yeah, I know. But it's not that simple. I don't love her and well, it just doesn't feel right to expect the marriage to be a marriage without it."

"Well, maybe you should court her?"

"*Court* her? She's my wife and besides—I don't want to love again. I just want what Janie needs and she needed a mother and now I've got myself into a pickle. I need a swift kick to the rear is what I need."

Jarred rubbed his jaw. "Seems to me you're thinking about Janie and yourself and you've forgotten a part of the vow you took."

Trey paused, his insides curled up like a tight fist. "What?" He had a feeling he wasn't about to like what the preacher had to say.

"The parts where you said vows about what you would do for your bride. For Lucy. She counts in this too, you know. And she's young and healthy. Are you expecting that she be a mother to Janie, clean and cook and never get anything in return?"

Trey groaned, not liking this at all. "As in what?" he asked warily.

"As in the chance to know love or at least the blessing of holding her own baby in her arms. To be loved and cherished."

He frowned in the dim light. "You are not helping my situation."

Jarred chuckled. "I'm just reminding you of your responsibilities and the vows you made before God. And I know you loved Beth with all your heart. But she would want you to be happy again. Sometimes, I've dealt with spouses who can't let themselves love again because they feel guilty about feeling love again. It's a normal emotion. But I've also learned that a heart is a wondrous thing and God created it with an unending capacity for love. Are you sure that's not what you're so upset about?"

Trey couldn't speak. He did feel guilty. He never thought about wanting someone else. He loved Beth with all his heart. She had been gone so long it sometimes seemed like life with her had just been a dream. And the worst part was every year that passed made it hard to remember all the special times, made it harder to remember what it felt like to be loved by her. He hated that. That right there added to his guilt for the fact that he found himself lying in bed, thinking about Lucy.

And now the preacher wasn't helping him by reminding him that he had made a promise to her. He'd vowed before God to love and cherish her.

His mouth grew dry as he stared at Jarred. "Seems like I've got some changes to do. In all of this, I haven't been thinking about Lucy at all. I've only been thinking about me and Janie…and Beth."

"Seems to me that someone ordered you a mail-order bride and you got blessed with a good one. I wouldn't take that for granted. I'll be praying for you."

"Thanks. And while we're on the subject, seems to me that a man like you could use a wife. Why are you always spending so much time out here staring up at the sky…you looking for answers too? Maybe someone needs to send off for a mail-order bride for you."

Jarred chuckled. "Believe me, I've thought about it. But I don't really know what the townfolks would think about if the preacher ordered himself a bride. I figure I'll let God remain in control of my love life. When the time is right, He'll bring the right woman along for me."

Trey shrugged and walked on home. He figured the good Lord worked in mysterious ways and might even use a mystery matchmaker to bring good wives into a man's life.

It had happened to him. Now he just had to figure out how to make it work.

By the time she heard Trey come into the house through the back entrance into the little storeroom, Lucy had almost fallen asleep. She got up and walked from the parlor through the kitchen. She then sucked in a deep breath and with fortitude, she tapped on his door.

He pulled the door open with the startled expression on his handsome face. “Lucy, you’re still up?”

He had untucked his shirt and he had removed his gun belt from his lean hips. She caught her breath and fought for bravery. Her mouth went dry. He didn’t help her situation at all. She felt breathless as she forced herself on. “I am still awake. I’ve been waiting for you. I wanted to let you know that this can’t go on. I feel horrible for taking your room and making you sleep on that cot.”

He frowned. “If we lived on a ranch, I’d probably be sleeping in the barn.”

“Oh, really?”

“Yes, really.”

She sighed. He’d defused her argument. She thought about it and then pushed herself to continue. “The truth is, I’m wondering…if this being a marriage of convenience is going to work. Janie is already asking about sleeping arrangements that are different than her friends'." She felt her cheeks heat up, especially by the bewildered expression on her new husband's face. She hadn't expected him to look as if he had no idea what she was talking about. "Oh, never mind. I'm going to bed." Turning away, she moved blindly away from him. Feelings she didn't quite understand struggled within her and tears stung her eyes. *How had she believed she could make this work?* The fact that she'd so quickly begun to long to feel her husband's strong arms around her was very nearly overwhelming. She questioned the sanity of willingly marrying a man who had no intention of ever loving her.

She'd not gone but a few steps when he called her name and moved in front of her to block her from running through the kitchen to her room.

"Lucy." He took her by the arms. "Look at me," he said when she kept her eyes down.

The last thing she wanted was for him to see the tears in her eyes.

"Are you crying?" he said, his voice husky as he gently placed a finger beneath her chin and lifted her face so he could see her better.

"N-no," she lied. She sniffed and blinked hard, hoping the dampness would disappear like dew in sunshine. And looking into his handsome face was like sunshine to her. Her heart tripped over itself at the look of tenderness she saw there.

"Please don't cry. I never meant to make you cry when I asked you to marry me and take care of Janie. It seems I've put you in a very hard situation. But one I hadn't fully thought out."

"Me?" she asked, looking up into his troubled eyes. She realized her hand was covering his heart and she could feel it beating rapidly, as was her own. And she was aware of his arms steadying her. She longed for him to kiss her and without thinking, her gaze dropped to his lips. When she looked back up at him, it was as if time had stopped. Her breath caught in her throat and, unable to stop herself, she leaned in to his body.

Instantly his hands tightened on her arms; then his arms were around her and he pulled her against him. "Yes, you," he whispered hoarsely. Then, to her delight, he lowered his head and brushed a tentative kiss against her lips.

Her heart hammered like the sound of a locomotive and her knees went weak. And then he deepened the kiss; his mouth settled fully on hers and everything in her world began to spin as emotions so strong and desires she'd never known flooded over her.

Suddenly he pulled away, his expression shocked. He took a step back; his arms dropped away from her and she stumbled. Her knees were so weak and suddenly without his support, she nearly sank to the floor. Thankfully the table was near and she steadied herself with a hand to its stout tabletop.

"I'm sorry," he said. "I—you need to go to bed."

"But—"

"Now," he bit out from tense lips. His voice was tight, gruff. He strode past her, through the storeroom and out the back door.

Breathless, and feeling as if her world had just begun and then been ripped away, Lucy ran to her room and closed the door behind her. She fell across the bed and cried.

What had she gotten herself into? He didn't want her. She'd seen the horror in his eyes, the disdain. His kiss had been beautiful and wonderful to her and it was obvious to her that her kiss for him had been horrible. She'd seen in his eyes how much she was lacking and he'd had the sudden realization that he'd hitched himself to a life with her and the idea, obviously hideous to him, had shown in his eyes.

What was she to do?

CHAPTER TWELVE

Trey leaned against the back of the house. He felt the most terrible sense of desolation and longing at the same time. It was daunting; staring at the stricken expression on Lucy's face killed him. But the emotions that had overwhelmed him prevented him from being able to take her back into his arms and assure her that everything was okay. Everything wasn't okay.

The guilt very nearly paralyzed him as he stared up at the dark sky. When he'd kissed Lucy, the most beautiful and unbelievable emotions had filled him.

Like Jarred had said, the guilt was there but the sense of betrayal had finally broken. Beth would want him to be happy. He knew it was so.

He closed his eyes and saw her sweet face and as if carried on the breeze, he thought he heard, “Good-bye, my love.” His eyes opened and he looked around but no one was there.

His heart pounded and he felt dazed. A sadness slammed into him and on its wings, the joy he’d felt while Lucy had been in his arms. *Lucy…* He wanted her back in his arms.

He wanted to make this farce of a wedding into a real marriage. A marriage like he and Beth had, built on love.

Wheeling around, he stomped back into the house…

Lucy was brokenhearted and mad. She paced her room and tried to think what she should do. It was obvious Trey didn’t want her and she could not endure this any longer. And yet she could not leave Janie. Could not bring herself to break the child's heart or the promise Lucy had made to her to be her mother.

What was she to do? She had really and truly gotten herself into a fix.

"Lucy." Trey calling her name softly at the door startled her.

Wiping the tears from her face, she stared at the door. Well, one thing was certain: if she was going to remain in the house with a man who could not love her, then at least she was not going to continue to act like a lovesick puppy. She would bury her feelings and start speaking her mind. And he could sleep on that hard cot all he wanted.

Unless he had come to claim the bed?

She had her nightgown on but didn't care. She stormed to the door and yanked it open. "What do you want?" she asked, keeping her voice down. She hiked her chin in the air and glared at him. She couldn't help it. She refused, absolutely refused, to cry anymore.

He stood still, his expression one of shock. His gaze ran down her and suddenly she wasn't so sure being in her nightgown had been a good idea.

Looking behind him, he moved into the room and she backed up a step. He closed the door behind him and tugged at his collar. "We need to talk."

"I'm tired. We've talked enough. I knew when we married what I was getting into. I just didn't realize you would never have a desire to…to love me. It would have been good to know that…but I will honor my commitment and love Janie and watch out for her. And as far as I'm concerned, I'll never mention your sleeping in here again. The lumpy cot is yours from here on out." She felt the tears despite being determined not to shed them. "I can't stand seeing the pain I saw in your eyes earlier. I can't put that there—"

He took a step toward her and she backed up one. She'd said her piece, all of it, and was determined to end it there.

"Lucy, I'm sorry. I just needed a moment. What you saw wasn't what you thought."

"What was it?" She sniffed.

"I've been struggling with letting Beth go. I've fallen in love with you, you see, and when I kissed you and opened my heart to what I've been feeling, I was overwhelmed. I didn't mean to hurt you."

Had she heard him correctly? He loved her?

"I love you, Lucy. From the day you came into my office and told me you were here to be my wife, my life changed. Your smiling face, big heart, and endearing spirit touched me. How can I not love you?"

Tears streamed down her face.

"Can you love me?"

Her knees were weak as she took a deep breath and nodded. "Oh yes. Always."

He smiled and swept her into his arms. He gently cupped her face with one of his large hands and then tenderly kissed her. "I will love you. And I'll cherish you, forever. So, can I come to bed?"

Her knees melted and he caught her up in his arms. She wrapped her arms around his neck and stared deeply into his golden-flecked eyes. "I love you," he said, as his eyes darkened with the same emotions that churned inside her. And then he kissed her and this time he didn't stop.

EPILOGUE

The next morning, as the pink streaks of the morning sunrise crept across the room and over the bed, Lucy woke, wrapped in Trey's arms. She felt well-loved and blissfully happy. *Had she dreamed the night before?* Never in her wildest imaginings had she known love was so beautiful and could be expressed…like that.

She sighed and snuggled against Trey, loving the feel of him beside her. She had taken a risk and followed her heart and it had led her here. And as Trey nuzzled her neck and pulled her close, she knew that it had all been worth it. This was exactly where she was supposed to be.

She just wondered who it was she owed a hug and a thank-you? And as Trey whispered, huskily in her ear, "Good morning Mrs. Jones," she knew she would forever be grateful to whomever her matchmaker was.

Don't miss THE PREACHER'S MAIL ORDER BRIDE the next story in the Mail-Order Brides of Sweet, Texas when Big John Wiggins, the six-foot-five-inch cupid strikes again. Pastor Jarred has no idea he's about to receive a package…one spunky mail-order bride!

Chapter Excerpt from

THE PREACHER'S MAIL ORDER BRIDE

Mail-Order Brides of Sweet, Texas Book Two

CHAPTER ONE

Huffing and puffing Mrs. Ambrosia Mulberry hustled toward the church, heading for the weekly quilting club meeting. She was late as she rounded the corner and ran straight into Pastor Andrews. She bumped right into the poor young man and bounced right off him. Thankfully her love of cherry scones and all things sweet had padded her figure enough that no harm was done. She chuckled when the handsome preacher reached to steady her.

"Oh, Mrs. Mulberry please forgive me. I wasn't watching where I was going. Are you all right?"

"Oh yes, yes, I'm fine. Here. Thankfully my treat for you was not squashed in our little calamity." She thrust the hatbox filled with the scones he loved at him and instantly was rewarded by his startlingly beautiful smile. It was an odd thing to think a man's smile was beautiful but there was no other way to describe Pastor Andrews's smile. Quite simply, handsome was not an adequate enough description.

"Why, Mrs. Mulberry, you're out to make me into a portly pastor. I'm on to your plan but unable to resist the temptation."

She beamed proudly as he pulled out a scone and right then and there popped it into his mouth.

"Pure bliss," he muttered happily as he chewed.

She loved that the young man loved the scones and it was the least she could do for the man of God. After all, she had to have some kind of ministry and this was just too easy but one she was well equipped to take on. Still, she wondered.

"You need a wife, Pastor Andrews. Someone who can bake and cook to your delight and be there at your side in your ministry."

It was true. He had been and would continue to be one of the topics of their quilting club. He gave and gave and never complained, but everyone noticed that he was always looking out for everyone and always went home to a dark house and a cold supper unless one of them took him something. They had even been considering sending off for a mail-order bride but they hadn't had the courage to do it. Why, everyone in town was still reeling from the fact that they had someone in their midst who was actually doing it…sending off for brides. Well, at least one so far but everyone was convinced that if the cupid would do it once, he or she would do it again.

At first, they all suspected a woman but they weren't sure. It could be a man. All the ladies had declared they hadn't done it. But that didn't mean all manner of townsfolk hadn't blamed it on them. After all, they were the ladies' quilting club, so for some strange reason that was enough to declare them the lead suspects.

Why, the sheriff and his new bride were living in wedded bliss since Lucy had come to town by false bait when someone had pretended to be Sheriff Trey when indeed it had not been him. It had all worked out but still, no one was talking and who had written the letters was still a secret.

Now she wondered who would be next. Because she felt it in her intuition that it was going to happen again. And soon.

As they stood there, the stagecoach roared into town. The grizzled driver, could be heard all the way to the church, yelling—

"Get the doctor! *The stage has been robbed and a passenger has been shot!"*

Jarred Andrews went on alert the instant he saw the stage rocking wildly as the driver barely controlled it into town. Hearing the old man's yells of alarm and Jarred instantly thrusting the scones at Mrs. Mulberry.

"Hold these please. I need to help." He raced to

offer aid.

The stage had come to a halt in front of Big John Wiggins's feed store. He crossed the short distance in a fast run and was at the old driver's side just as he yanked opened the door.

It was a woman.

"She's a tiny thing but tough. Told that bandit he couldn't have what she had in her bag and when he tried to take it, she walloped him on the head with a metal rod she had hidden within her skirt. So he shot her."

Jarred was half listening to the tale as he entered the stagecoach and found the poor woman crumpled on the floor, where she'd probably fallen off the seat when the driver raced over the rough terrain to get her here.

Her shoulder was bleeding and he quickly stripped off his suit coat and tried to stanch the bleeding. She groaned as he pressed down, but he'd learned when he'd been in the war that bleeding needed pressure to stop it.

"Someone get the doctor," he yelled out the door. Then he gathered her in his arms so that he could take her to the doc's if he needed to.

She cried out and her eyes opened. Jarred's heart stopped as he gazed into eyes the color of the first blues of a morning sunrise. His steps faltered momentarily and then he moved forward and out down the steps.

"Pastor, the doc's delivering a baby out at the Murrys'," Big John Wiggins said. "But his office is open. Come on."

Jarred had tended to a lot of bullet wounds but didn't do that anymore. He'd done it because the military had thrust him at it but it wasn't something he enjoyed. Taking a bullet out hurt and he didn't like hurting people. Quite the contrary; a pastor liked offering comfort.

But if it would save a life or was a last resort and there was no way out…

There was a large entourage as he strode around the corner to the doc's office. He waited while Big

John pushed the door open and then he carried her inside. He strode to the examination table and placed her there.

She groaned and her eyes flickered open. She mumbled something and he didn't understand. She tried again and he leaned close to hear as she whispered, "He didn't get it, did he?"

Mail-Order Brides of Sweet, Texas Series

The Lawman's Mail Order Bride, Book 1

The Preacher's Mail Order Bride, Book 2

The Rancher's Mail Order Bride, Book 3

The Cowboy’s Mail Order Bride, Book 4

About the Author

Elizabeth Chasen loves to write 'hopeful' romantic stories that inspire and entertain. All of her books are clean and wholesome Christian romance. She finds joy in bringing her fun characters to life and giving each of her couples their happy ending!

Always fascinated by Mail Order Bride historical romance, she enjoys creating her own stories to bring to her readers. Mail Order Brides of Sweet, Texas is the first of many series to come, so enjoy and she invites you to join her mailing list so you'll be the first to hear when her next exciting historical western romance is releasing. Just go to: ww.elizabethchasen.blogspot.com. Happy reading!

www.ingramcontent.com/pod-product-compliance
Lightning Source LLC
Chambersburg PA
CBHW070500170726
48291CB00008B/2582
9781949492668